Santa Fe

in the

Fifties

A Memoir of Change in the
City Different during the Postwar Era

SANTA FE

in the

Fifties

A Memoir of Change in the
City Different during the Postwar Era

----

by Violet A. Kochendoerfer

WESTERN EDGE PRESS

ISBN: 1-889921-07-6

LC: 98 061163

Western Edge Press
126 Candelario Street
Santa Fe, New Mexico 87501

505/988-7214
westernedge@santa-fe.net

Edited by Ann Mason

Designed by Jim Mafchir

All photographs by Violet A. Kochendoerfer unless otherwise noted.

Cover photo: Looking toward La Fonda Hotel during Fiesta.

Frontispiece: Violet Kochendoerfer in front of sandstone formations
outside of Abiquiu, shortly after she arrived in Santa Fe.

FIRST EDITION

CONTENTS

Santa Fe

in the

Fifties

A Memoir of Change in the
City Different during the Postwar Era

Violet sets out for a new life in Santa Fe.

INTRODUCTION

Decisions! How they determine our lives! If I had accepted an invitation to visit Berkeley in the late 1940s from Elsie Semrau, an American Red Cross friend of World War II days, I would not have moved to the Land of Enchantment. I would never have called the romantic City Different home or known the wonders of experiencing Old World culture in the New World, as I belatedly learned about the early history of the Southwest long before the Pilgrims landed at Plymouth Rock. And I would never have shared a unique art world, been intrigued by the wisdoms of the Pueblo Indian culture, or have known the dreams of pioneers like Mabel Dodge Luhan and her coterie of friends, including D. H. Lawrence and Georgia O'Keeffe.

I was raised in Minnesota as a Missouri Synod Lutheran in a lower middle-class family. For most girls, including my friends, the goal after graduating from high school was to marry a man and raise a family. But that wasn't my choice. Although at the time I had no dreams of exploring the world or developing great talents, I had taken a commercial course because it offered the kinds of skills necessary for women to find employment. I graduated as salutatorian of my 1929 high school class and did get a good position as secretary to the president of Winona State Teachers College.

I enjoyed the college atmosphere at work and spent a lot of my spare time at the YWCA, where a secretary changed my direction. Edna Buckley kept insisting I go to college and finally convinced me. Because I'd envied students at WSTC who could come home for the holidays, I decided to

3

find a college in Portland, Oregon, where I had relatives. A Winona professor reinforced that decision by telling me about Portland's Reed College. Rather than teach from textbooks, Reed's goal was for students to learn how to think for themselves, with the aid of long reading lists and much personal interaction with faculty.

After inquiring about attending Reed, I was informed that with the $1,800 I'd saved, I could make it through if I worked on campus; but they were wrong. Although my money lasted only two years, I was offered a job as assistant to a new dean of men, Easton Rothwell, who became my mentor for the rest of his life. Even though he held high positions and knew important people around the world, he made me also feel important. But when he took a leave of absence for a State Department assignment I questioned the values of his temporary replacement and resigned to become the first employee of the wartime Office of Price Administration.

I began as junior stenographer at $1,440 a year with the proviso that I could have any job I could handle. As secretary to the newly appointed OPA Oregon State director, I helped open district offices and was put in charge of personnel. When the OPA offices in the Portland Bedell Building grew from two rooms to two floors and my salary went up to $8,000, the district office said, "We want a man!" Their man came—a typewriter was put back on my desk, and again I resigned.

At that time coincidentally the Women's Army Auxiliary Corps was being formed; and against my better judgment but with a feeling of rebellion I enrolled. After basic training, I was given instruction as a Morse code radio operator and sent to Morris Field in North Carolina. Because we were not legally in the Army, we could not operate on the Army Airways Communications Net and had to be trained as link trainer instructors. Nine months later, when the WAAC became the Women's Army Corps, I refused to enlist for two years.

World War II was in progress, and I applied for overseas service with the American Red Cross, sailing Easter Sunday of 1944 on the *Queen Mary*. I spent the next three and a half years as director of military service clubs in the European Theater, dodging buzz bombs on an airbase in England and leaving for the Continent after D-Day.

There, as senior club director for the 82nd Airborne, I participated in the historic crossing of the Elbe River; the liberation of a concentration camp, as the 21st German Army surrendered to our General Gavin; and celebrations with the Russians, toasting Stalin as they toasted President Roosevelt, who had just died.

When the 82nd Division occupied Berlin, I was a dinner guest of General Dwight Eisenhower, and concluded my overseas time directing three leave clubs at Garmisch-Partenkirchen in the Bavarian Mountains. My story of those years, entitled *One Woman's World War II*, was published for the fiftieth anniversary of D-Day.

Then, after the war, I returned to my family home in Minnesota. But after a few months of catching up with family and exclaiming over babies of hometown friends, there seemed little to talk about. I knew this was not where I wanted to stay.

Although I seriously considered my Red Cross friend Elsie's invitation to come to Berkeley, I realized that because I disliked big cities it might not be wise to move to the Bay Area of California. So instead I decided to select a smaller community in a part of the country I had yet to explore.

Then I remembered a letter I had received from a hometown friend while in Bavaria during World War II, in which she had described a visit to Audrey, a mutual hometown friend who had moved to Santa Fe and married a Spanish man. She remarked, "When you'd write about Garmisch-Partenkirchen, Vi—that picture-book village of chalets surrounded by protecting mountains—I just knew you'd love

Santa Fe."

I immediately wrote Audrey, who quickly replied that she loved Santa Fe and hoped she'd never have to live anywhere else, adding that it would be great to have another Minnesota friend there. Her enthusiasm, along with her offer of a room until I got settled, was the necessary impetus to move to Santa Fe. Excitedly, I started making plans and packing things I would take with me to start a new life, never dreaming of the many new relationships and extraordinary cultural experiences the next ten years would bring.

CHAPTER I

- -

From D-Day to the City
Different

In moving to Santa Fe, I felt both rebellious and adventurous. I was running away from my hometown, in which I had two still-single high school boyfriends; but even though I had lived in England, France, and Germany, there was so much of my own country to explore. Making a living did not concern me since I knew that with my secretarial experience I could land a good job almost anywhere.

To buy a new Ford or Chevrolet in the late 1940s, you had to get on a waiting list. But I was eager to begin my new life; and when my garage man brought out a used Studebaker Landcruiser, I bought it. In early November 1948, I left for Santa Fe in a car every collector well remembers. Studebaker pioneered today's design with its Landcruiser's trunk space in the rear, which looked similar to the front hood. People back then said, "You can't tell whether it's coming or going!"

I had made no effort to learn about my destination. Travel agencies didn't cram the Yellow Pages back then, and all I had was a road map to lead me to a part of the country far from Minnesota's more than ten thousand blue lakes, carpets of green lawns, and the shade of innumerable trees. I had actually envisioned the Southwest as a desert country. So when I crossed into New Mexico on the north from Colorado through the forested mountains of Raton Pass I was unbelieving. Excitement grew as I drove through Taos. There were no Minnesota wood or brick homes with shingled roofs, no thatched-roof cottages or historic buildings of Europe. Houses and downtown store buildings were all of brown earth! Even the people were different—some almost in costume! In a dis-

7

arming experience of discovery, I was entering a whole new world I'd never learned about even in school.

On the way south to Santa Fe, I stopped at a small town named Tesuque, wondering just how to pronounce it. I'd begun to reflect on the odd spelling on signs I'd seen along the way. A man in Tesuque explained how I could enter Santa Fe on the street that would take me right to the Plaza, which is what their town square was called. Surprisingly, the Plaza had green grass like parks back home with four paths leading from corners to a central monument. It was surrounded by more brown earthen storefronts on three sides, while the fourth was a long porch-like structure which extended the entire block and was held up by large solid posts. Later, I learned it was the Palace of the Governors—the oldest governmental building in our country.

I waited at that corner to take it all in and then asked directions for Canyon Road, where my friend Audrey lived. I was told, "Just drive out Palace Avenue here to the left. The Post Office will be on the right at the first corner. That's Cathedral Place. The next will be Castillo, with the empty lot on the right corner, where the big new hospital will be built. Turn right there and go a long block till you cross the Alameda, the street which runs all along the little Santa Fe River. Keep straight across the river, and just over the bridge you'll find the road turns a bit to the left. That's Canyon Road. What number do you want—909? That'll be pretty far out on your left. You'll drive along a lot of adobe buildings; but look for the number on the wall."

That early evening on Canyon Road I was passed by two cars on what seemed like a country lane. I drove into a strange world of brown earthen buildings on both sides of the road— walls or fences without doors and hardly any windows. I noticed a little storefront back off the road with a porch-like structure where colorful wares were shelved, but I saw no sidewalks or green lawns. Human life here seemed hidden, and I wondered what was behind all those brown walls.

Finally, I spotted number 909 on shiny colored tiles set high in an adobe wall on the left. Just above the number were two small sunken windows that made me realize the thickness of the adobe walls. Connected to the house was a high adobe wall with a wrought-iron gate. It opened into a delightful little walled patio, with a carpet of green grass crossed by a flagstone walkway that led up to the door of the house Audrey shared with her husband, Alfred Baca, a native of Santa Fe.

I was excited as I entered my first adobe home. Part of a poem I later sent to friends describes a few surprises that awaited me in colorful, unconventional old Santa Fe:

I loved the old adobe house with two foot thick the wall,
And ceilings high with *vigas;* but wait, that's still not all!
Two doors there in the kitchen, much like out on the farm,
One could be boys' the other girls' but that's a false alarm.
It's really only one for both, you've got to lock the door.
Inside the john's a dilly, like you've never seen before.
It's red with all the trimmings; you've never seen the beat;
Put down the cover and you'll see sunflowers on the seat!
And as you sit there looking down to shiny turquoise floor,
You'll see two bright red footprints. You guess what they are for!
And in the great big living room there's a corner fireplace
That burns the perfumed piñon that warms your feet and face.

The poem went on to describe how high ceilings were held up by cross beams as big as telephone poles, called *vigas.* It also explained that Audrey worked for an architect who had

planned the town of Los Alamos, where the first atomic bomb
had been built, and that Audrey and her Spanish husband Al
had arranged trips to introduce me to my new surroundings.

One trip was north to Taos on what was to become my
favorite backroad through many little Spanish towns, including
Cordova, Truchas, and Las Trampas. Now known as the High
Road to Taos, it twisted along the crest of high rolling hills
dotted with piñons, from which we could see down on either
side. On the way back down Highway 64, I tried reading
Spanish signs, learning from Al and Audrey to pronounce *j* like
an *h* and double *ll*s like a *y*. They smiled as I had trouble pro-
nouncing a sign saying "Doughbilly" until I realized it wasn't
Spanish!

One evening I was introduced to El Nido (The Nest)—a
cozy nightspot north of the city. Another memorable evening
Al taught me how to make Santa Fe enchiladas the old-fashioned way using blue corn tortillas, which looked for all the
world like circles cut out of gray-blue automobile inner
tubes—before the time of tubeless tires. Al went on to describe
the finer culinary points: "You fry a tortilla in hot fat till it crin-
kles like this, and put it on this special plate with the straight
lip around to hold the chile sauce. Sprinkle it with grated
cheese and chopped onion. Spoon over chile. Then you do
another tortilla and repeat this till it's as high as you want.
Spoon a lot of chile over the whole thing and put it in the oven
for all the stuff to melt together. Then you serve it with a fried
egg on top. That's the Santa Fe signature."

I also learned a lot of local history from native-born Al, who
made sure I understood my place in the tricultural mix of the
area: "You're an *Anglo*, Vi, and believe it or not, you could even
be a *gringo* if they don't like you much. But the truth is that
the first Anglos to come to Santa Fe were prisoners, and they
came under military guard. That was just a few years before the
twenty-first anniversary of our city, which the Spanish founded
in 1609.

"It all happened when a small group of U.S. explorers acci-

- -

dentally wandered into what was then the Spanish Empire. That was the winter of 1805. They had orders from President Thomas Jefferson to find the sources of western tributaries of the Mississippi River. Without knowing it they stumbled upon the headwaters of the Rio Grande in the Colorado Rockies. That's where they were arrested by the Spanish militia and brought down here for questioning."

I was fascinated to learn about historic events of centuries ago about which I had never been told in school; so I kept urging Al to go on. He continued, "Well, if you're talking about New Mexico history, Vi, they say it goes back even to prehistory—would you believe to 1200 B.C. with cave dwellers here in southern and western New Mexico. And our Pueblo Indians go back to at least A.D. 1300.

"Then in the early 1500s, around Michelangelo's time, a few Spaniards survived a shipwreck, and we began to hear about what they called New Spain, which is present-day Mexico. There were legends of the Seven Cities of Gold, and that's when old Coronado came north looking for these cities. He didn't find the gold, but did find people living in mud houses.

"In about 1500, Spain started colonizing, and put a guy called Juan de Oñate in charge. He started the first European settlement at San Gabriel, up near our San Juan Pueblo about twenty-five miles north of here. He also brought along a lot of Franciscan friars, who got busy building fifty-some churches, trying to convert the Tewas in the pueblos.

"Don Pedro de Peralta was the third governor, and he moved the capital here to a spot that had originally been a Pueblo village. There's a story that an Indian legend called it 'The Dancing Ground of the Sun,' and I like to think of our Plaza that way. Anyway, Peralta built the Palace of the Governors and made Santa Fe the oldest capital in the U.S.

"But his people were pretty brutal in their repression of the traditional Pueblo ways and didn't try to understand their culture or religion. The Spanish repression brought on continual conflict, and in 1680 the Indians rebelled. The Spaniards had to

---

flee south to what's now Juarez in Mexico. The Pueblos took over and moved into the Palace of the Governors. But they were basically not a fighting people, and in 1692, after thirteen years there was a takeover without much resistance by Governor-General Don Diego de Vargas.

"That put the Spanish back in rule; and because they allowed no foreign trade, Santa Fe was practically isolated from the rest of the world for a couple hundred years. But it was during this terrible isolation that the distinctive New Mexico weaving and religious art developed—the kind that's so special today. Then, in 1821, even though New Mexico won its political independence from Spain, the Spanish culture and influence of early settlers and explorers lingered on and still play a major role in Santa Fe today.

"That's when 'new' with a small *n* came into being. The new Mexican government broke with the long Spanish isolation and wanted to get to know its neighbors to the northeast. Supposedly it started when some Mexican militia from Santa Fe ran into a bunch of Missourians trading with the Indians. It caught on, and a guy by the name of Bucknell brought stuff in from Missouri by the wagonload. That was the beginning of the Old Santa Fe Trail, and for the next fifty years thousands of Anglos traversed the trail. This commerce helped create jobs and a lot of income each year for both the Spanish and the Americans. But it also led to a twenty-year war with Mexico.

"President Polk started that war back in the 1840s. He had hoped to expand our U.S. influence all the way to the Pacific Ocean. Santa Fe was on the way so he used it as an important U.S. Army post. But the U.S. soldiers hated Santa Fe. To them it was a filthy place built of mud, which they called 'the Siberia of America.' They felt a good home was one built of milled lumber or brick with a pitched, shingled roof like theirs.

"Then in 1912 New Mexico became a state. Although lots of adobe building did go on, for some there was a bit of compromise. Adobe walls were crowned along roof lines with fancy layers of brick. Some had windows and portals and even Greek

Revival doors. They called this the Territorial style, which you'll see a lot of in Santa Fe."

I could tell Al was proud of his Spanish heritage, and I felt fortunate to experience his cultural and historical insights and sharing. After all, it was his people who had come to this land of the Native American Indian before we arrived; but we both now felt part of the white race and seemed to be pretty accepting of each other. With less than 1 percent blacks and 2 percent Native American Indians, I realized it was up to us whether we were viewed by Al's people as Anglos or gringos. History came alive for me with the thought of how much I could contribute, although I realized I still had much to learn about the exciting early history of my country.

One day a couple weeks after I had arrived, a person who heard I'd been overseas with the Red Cross during World War II said, "Have you met Gloria at Sears? She was a Red Crosser, too, and she's now in charge of personnel there." Naturally, I stopped in to see her, and we had much to talk about. Gloria, who had not been overseas, was deeply impressed as I shared my World War II experiences. She then said, "Vi, have you ever sold hosiery or purses? I desperately need someone. Can you help me out?" That was back when they had a clerk at each counter. Although I wanted to find a secretarial job, I realized that with little industry, and with mainly the Capitol and State Penitentiary as potential job locations, there weren't too many possible places of employment. So until I got settled I accepted the job as saleswoman, which paid $5.00 a day plus 1 percent commission on sales.

I needed a place to live, and with Al's help found a little adobe guest house behind the big home at 359 Garcia Street just off Canyon Road. Santa Feans built such separate living arrangements on their property—complete with cooking facilities—to accommodate their many visitors.

I wrote family that my Santa Fe home looked like an adobe two-car garage without the big doors, and only one small window on either side. It had an adequate kitchen area and a bath with shower. You entered the large living area with a pull-down bed at one end across from a small corner kiva fireplace.

After moving in clothes, books, a favorite rattan chair with red cushions, and three lamps I'd brought from Minnesota, plus loans from Audrey and Al, it began to look like home. There was even a tiny Christmas tree, which we had gone to the woods to get. I now had my own address and became a valid Santa Fe resident near that historic part of town I'd felt to be so mysterious only a few weeks before.

CHAPTER 2

Working at the Chamber of Commerce

After Christmas of 1948, my first priority was to find more suitable and permanent work, and in searching I discovered that jobwise Santa Fe was truly the City Different. It was the oldest state capital in our country, and once given the choice between being home to the state university or the state penitentiary it had chosen the pen. Consequently, since Santa Fe had small shops rather than big businesses, most prospects were government jobs, which I had always avoided.

Even so, with my good secretarial experience, and with friends like Al and Audrey, I did not have to worry—just wonder where the new job would be. Audrey had a top position with Willard C. Kruger, the architect who had helped build Los Alamos for the Manhattan Project, which focused on constructing the first atomic bomb. After talking with her, I wrote off a government job in Santa Fe and became more interested in Los Alamos as an exciting history-making part of my new location.

My excitement increased when I applied at a personnel office they had in Prince Plaza and found that a top secretarial job at Los Alamos would require an FBI "Q" clearance, which would take about three months. A week later when I went back to say I needed some kind of work to tide me over, the woman in charge said, "Well, let's see if we can find something unclassified until the clearance comes through." The next day she called to tell me the Santa Fe Chamber of Commerce needed some temporary help. I agreed to go and quit my clerking job at Sears.

I was asked to begin work at the Chamber of Commerce one

15

evening at 7:00 since they were behind schedule producing a brochure designed to attract the administrative offices of the Atomic Energy Commission, which was planning to move from Los Alamos.

Early the next morning I reported for work once again. As I walked into the attractive adobe building on Shelby Street, Jim Riley, the secretary-manager, was tearing his hair out, saying, "I gave Anna notes for a 9:30 meeting this morning, and she hasn't come in! She asked to get off early last night and promised to come in early after Mass to transcribe her notes. Now what'll I do?" I said, "If you can find her shorthand, I'll see if I can read it and get out some kind of report." This idea helped. Subsequently, we found out she'd taken off for California to attend a family funeral. She never did return, and Jim asked whether I'd stay on until they could find someone to replace her—someone who knew Santa Fe and could answer all the tourists' questions. I agreed.

Sometime later Jim asked whether I'd consider staying on permanently, and I told him I'd have to think about it since the salary wasn't anything to write home about. After a while Jim made me a better offer, saying, "I know I can up that salary. I'll just have to check it out with the board." As a result, I didn't wait for the FBI clearance and stayed in Santa Fe at the Chamber of Commerce.

Another woman already worked at the Chamber of Commerce. Ann Baumann handled the heavy load of mailings. Among other promotional letters, we would get hundreds from schoolchildren around the country saying they were studying New Mexico and asking for information. To better handle such requests, I wrote and had published a brochure with some simple state history and other facts, including information about the state bird, the roadrunner; the state flower, the yucca; the state tree, the piñon, or pine nut; the state gem, turquoise; the state vegetables, chile and pinto beans; the state seal, two eagles representing the annexation of New Mexico to the United States; and the state flag, a stylized red sun on a yellow field (symbol of Zia Pueblo Indians).

Ann was the daughter of the respected Santa Fe artist Gustave Baumann, whose specialty was wood block prints. His work consisted of basswood woodcuts of American rural landscapes and experiences in colorful hand-ground pigments. I was to learn later how famous he was to become.

After his death in 1971, his unique work received international acclaim. The Museum of New Mexico Press published *Gustave Baumann: Nearer to Art*, containing 124 of his prints "awash in brilliant hand-ground pigments, simple and elegant studies rooted in an America that manages to be both delicate and rugged, personal and mythic."

In an August 1994 letter, Ann wrote about her father's growing posthumous recognition: "Enclosed is a press release (issued last September) regarding the first comprehensive book on my father, which was published in connection with a big exhibit last fall. The book has generated a lot of interest in Baumann, and suddenly I'm finding myself involved in copyright matters. I hold the underlying copyright on all Baumann work in existence as well as working with the author on another book concerned with how Baumann made a color wood block print. This means trying to find material my father wrote re this subject. I have all his papers still.

"Also, a fine publisher of reproductions of artwork in the form of posters, calendars, notecards, etc., has contacted me re doing a calendar for 1996 and future projects. We're now in the process of negotiating a contract in connection with the Fine Arts Museum since it is work from their Baumann collection that will be used."

Back in the 1950s, I was more enamored with Baumann's imaginative marionettes. I fondly remember watching shows in a little theater with a big stage at their home at 409 Camino de las Animos, which Gustave had designed and built. Performances featuring his many eight- to twelve-inch marionettes always delighted us. I was often a guest at the Baumanns and recall a Thanksgiving Day dinner when we offered thanks with hands joined all around the table.

In 1951, Ann left the Chamber of Commerce and traveled to

New York for a brief stay before going to California to work for the American Friends Service Committee. She still lives in California, involved with handling her father's legacy so his work can be seen by appreciative people around the world. About twenty-five years ago her mother gave the marionettes to the New Mexico Museum of Fine Arts in Santa Fe, which has found someone who can operate them in a memorable way, and is restoring them for use in special programs during the Christmas season.

By the time my FBI clearance to work at Los Alamos came through, I was already pleased with my interesting job at the Chamber of Commerce and happy to be a Santa Fe resident. Consequently, I never worked at Los Alamos. However, I'm delighted to still have the document as a great conversation piece! It is a half-inch-thick historic document from which I learned things about myself and even my family I never knew— gleaned from interviews with relatives and anyone I had ever known, gone to school or worked with, or lived next to. At one point the FBI had found what they thought was my signature on a questionable political petition when I was a student at Reed College in Portland, Oregon—a problem requiring clearance between four FBI offices. I stayed at the Chamber of Commerce.

The Chamber of Commerce was located only a quarter of a block from the Santa Fe Plaza across Shelby Street from the historic La Fonda Hotel. From where I lived on Garcia Street, I could walk to work at the attractive building, which is no longer there. An adobe with a big plate-glass window in front, the building's entrance was through a wrought-iron gate in the adobe wall that enclosed a flagstoned patio. The small glass panes in the office door were painted in colorful folk art designs, a typical Santa Fe decoration that seemed to express pride in a Spanish heritage.

Seeing La Fonda Hotel as I came to work each day took me back to the historic past. I was fascinated with the La Fonda story, for it was established on its present site adjacent to the Plaza before the opening of the Santa Fe Trail. At the time of

----

the American occupation in 1846, the first small inn at this site was the U.S. Hotel, where guests paid a dollar a day for room and board, even though they sometimes had to sleep on or under the billiard tables in the lobby if the town was crowded. The present building was constructed in 1920 but has been enlarged several times since then. When its original designers ran short of money, it was sold to the Fred Harvey Company, one of the earliest large-scale promoters of western tourism.

In the 1950s, it was still a Fred Harvey hotel. On the cover of a brochure I picked up in the lobby, it was described as the "center of the most interesting hundred-mile square in America." The brochure continued:

> Facing the centuries-old Plaza, on the site of the original fonda of wagon-train days, La Fonda sweeps back in earth-colored terraces like those of its neighboring Indian pueblos. It's the greatest place imaginable in which to indulge neglected whims. Lose yourself in the care-free camaraderie of the unique hotel that's not like a hotel at all—where Old World charm and city sophistication mingle in an intriguing new pattern. For an utterly different vacation, come to La Fonda in Old Santa Fe.
>
> Each of La Fonda's quiet rooms has its individual decoration treatment, the furnishings including rare pieces from Spain and Mexico. Fred Harvey cuisine, internationally renowned for its quality, flavor and variety, adds to La Fonda's fame as one of America's finest hotels. There is a delightful cocktail room (La Cantina), a lovely outdoor dining place (La Placita), a fascinating Indian and Mexican shop, a newsstand (carrying a wide selection of books on Indian culture, the Southwest, etc.), a barber shop and beauty shop.
>
> Rates—European Plan—(all with bath) Single $4 to $8; Double $6.50 to $12; Twin beds $7 to $12; Living Room Suites $22 to $35; Table d'hote service—Breakfast $.60 & up; Luncheon $.85 & up; Dinner $2 & up; Camida Corrida Mexicana (Complete Mexican Dinner) $2.50. A la carte service at moderate prices. Music during

luncheon. Dancing in the quaint New Mexican Room at dinner and in the evening, with Mexican Orchestra playing for dancing and singing native folk songs.

That historic building remained part of my workdays since the Chamber of Commerce employees would go there for coffee breaks, or to have a drink with one of our business friends. Buck Riordan, the Albuquerque representative of TWA came to Santa Fe each week when TWA was one of four airlines which serviced Santa Fe at that time.There were also Continental, Pioneer, and Mohawk; but I recall a letter from the president of Pioneer saying that if we didn't keep the cattle off the runway, they'd have to think twice about coming to Santa Fe. Consequently, I did hire a man to check fences and make sure runways were clear of cattle. Today there is no major airline service to Santa Fe.

The extensive responsibilities and activities of the Chamber of Commerce were summed up one day in an article in the daily newspaper the *Santa Fe New Mexican,* headlined Your Chamber of Commerce Makes Santa Fe Its Business. It said:

> **Tourism.** Thousands of tourists each year visit the Chamber seeking accommodations, information on points of interest, things to do, historical data, road information and many other subjects. **New Business.** Hundreds of letters are answered and conferences held with persons seeking information regarding business opportunities. **New Residents.** Thousands of letters are received from many who have visited Santa Fe and feel it a desirable place to live. **Community Projects.** Dozens seek the support of the Chamber as it investigates others for the purpose of improving economic conditions, stabilization of property values and job security for the resident. **Community host.** Each year Congressional delegations, nationally and internationally-known personalities and dozens of groups of school children come to Santa Fe for business or pleasure. **Conventions.** Works to attract a calendar of conventions to Santa Fe, assisting

with planning, entertainment and needs of delegates coming. **Community Advertising** in national publications, providing historical information and photographs and arranging personal interviews. Has promoted Santa Fe as the location for the **Filming of Motion Pictures,** assisting in such productions which leave tens of thousands of dollars in the community. **Information.** Acts as question-answering center by mail, telephone and personal interview to strangers, local residents and businessmen many times each day.

At the Chamber of Commerce, I was to experience all these activities and found they weren't exaggerating when they mentioned thousands of pieces of mail to be answered. Jim handled the business affairs, but since there was no visitors' center as there now is across from the Pink Adobe restaurant, our office acted as the visitors' center.

I immediately wrote and had published three brochures to use in mailings—*This Is Santa Fe for the Visitor, This Is Santa Fe for the New Resident,* and *This Is Santa Fe for the Student.* Researching facts for the pamphlets connected me with my new town and made me eager to share with potential visitors my enthusiasm about its ancient, colorful tricultural history.

The cover of each pamphlet had a sketch of the Palace of the Governors, a large kachina doll, and a short history about the Ancient city—Santa Fe (La Villa Real de la Santa Fe de San Francisco de Assisi), founded in 1610 by Don Pedro de Peralta. I felt that this condensed history was important to those who were to be involved with us in any way.

The first section of *This Is Santa Fe for the Visitor* pertained to history and said:

Coming to Santa Fe is like coming to another world, for there is no city in the United States to compare in romance and history. You will be fascinated by its ancient narrow streets lined by brown adobe houses with their picturesque patios, the towering cottonwoods, the fragrance of piñon smoke, the music of spoken Spanish, the colorful dress of the Indians from the neighboring pueblos. All these are a part of Old Santa Fe which lies nestled at the foot of the Sangre de Cristo Mountains overlooking the Rio Grande Valley in the Land of Enchantment— a land of vast distances and deep color.

For those coming for the first time, there was additional information about the historic Plaza and the Palace of the Governors, which then housed the Museum of New Mexico, the School of American Research, and the Historical Society of New Mexico. The brochure then continued about what to see at that time in the 1950s:

> On the northwest corner of the Plaza is the NEW MEXICO MUSEUM OF ART, the first art museum in the United States, built in 1917 in the Spanish pueblo tradition. It houses a fine collection of Southwestern art, and is a "must" when you visit Santa Fe. One block east of the Governor's Palace are SENA AND PRINCE PLAZAS, built as homes of the old Sena family, and later the home of Governor Bradford Prince, one of the best-known territorial governors. These plazas were the centers of social life in early days. Although many rooms are now converted into offices and fascinating little shops, in exploring the charming patios you will feel the lingering flavor of antiquity.
>
> Just off the Plaza at the head of San Francisco Street (named after the patron saint of Santa Fe) is the CATHEDRAL OF ST. FRANCIS, an imposing structure of pink limestone with Romanesque lines, which was planned and built by Archbishop Lamy in 1869 to serve the needs of the Spanish people in New Mexico. He lies buried in the crypt behind the altar which dominates the interior.
>
> Every visitor to Santa Fe asks to see the OLDEST CHURCH, the MISSION OF SAN MIGUEL, which was built for the use of Indian slaves of the Spanish officials about 1636. Across the lane from the Mission is THE OLD HOUSE built of puddled adobe, and believed to be pre-Spanish in part of its construction.

Coming back to the Plaza from the Mission, one passes OUR LADY OF LIGHT CHAPEL at LORETTO ACADEMY, which houses the MIRACULOUS STAIR-CASE. For a time the chapel was without a staircase to the choir. Difficulty in construction had caused workmen to abandon the task, and it was left unfinished until an unknown carpenter appeared and completed a circular staircase, which has no visible means of support, and which was built without the use of a nail. Legend identifies the carpenter with St. Joseph.

In another direction from the Plaza is GUADALUPE CHURCH, the spiritual and social center of a very old section of Santa Fe. It is named for the Virgin of Guadalupe, the patron saint of Mexico around whom the famous legend has grown. The original painting of Our Lady of Guadalupe hangs above the tall altar. A little further out is the CHURCH OF SANTO ROSARIO, which is said to be a part of the chapel De Vargas raised in his camp after his reentry into Santa Fe in 1692, La Conquistadora (the image which De Vargas brought with him at the time, and to which he credited his victory) is carried annually to this church from the Cathedral and left for one week.

In making a long drive out Canyon Road, one of the oldest streets in Santa Fe, and along which many artists now live, is CRISTO REY CHURCH, the largest adobe structure in the nation because it was designed to house the world famous *reredos* (art walls behind the altar) carved from native stone and dating back to 1761. Turning off Canyon Road on Camino del Monte Sol (Road of the Sun Mountain), one passes homes of LOS CINCO PINTORES (the five painters) who founded Santa Fe's famed art reputation, the LABORATORY OF ANTHROPOLOGY (a scientific and educational institution dedicated to research in all phases of human achievement in the Southwest from earliest prehistoric times), and THE MUSEUM OF NAVAJO CEREMONIAL ART, where within a modern interpretation of a Navajo Ceremonial Hogan displays the most important collection of reproductions of the Navajo sandpaintings. Returning to the Plaza on the OLD PECOS ROAD, you follow the route over which the OLD SANTA FE TRAIL entered the city.

In connection with my research for the Chamber of Commerce pamphlets, I continued to learn more fascinating details about Santa Fe's history, beginning in the 1500s when the Spanish conquistadors came to shape the New World in the image of the Old World on behalf of "God, gold, and glory." But they ran into difficulties that brought them little gold or glory as they encountered the Pueblo Indians in the Royal City of the Holy Faith of St. Francis.

Some of these early colonists were apostolic priests involved with flagellation rites still practiced in northern New Mexico. After a severe drought in the 1670s, the Spanish governor decided to obliterate all traces of Pueblo religion. Many of the Indians had accepted Catholicism, but only as a supplement to their traditional beliefs, which they never considered giving up. As a result, this governor tried forty-seven Pueblo shamans for sorcery and hung three. One of those released was a powerful leader named Popé, who organized a resurrection against the Spanish by persuading the various pueblos to simultaneously carry out his plan, ultimately resulting in the well-known Pueblo Revolt of 1680.

The revolt began in the individual pueblos and eventually spread to Santa Fe, where Spanish survivors barricaded themselves in the Palace of the Governors, which they occupied for twelve years. Originally the structure extended much farther north and west than at present, with no portal, and had defense towers on each side facing the present Plaza.

For twelve years the Pueblo Indians occupied the Palace of the Governors and transformed the Plaza area into a typical pueblo. Some of the small Spanish windows and doors were blocked up, and rooms were entered from the top by ladders. Like Taos Pueblo the structure grew upward, probably to three or four stories high. One of the defense towers was converted into a ceremonial chamber, which the returning Spanish later reluctantly used for their own worship until they completed a new parish church. Finally in 1692, when the viceroy of New Spain sent Don Diego de Vargas to Santa Fe, he returned without resistance from the Pueblos.

Historically, the Plaza always remained the community center and marketplace for produce of the Rio Grande Valley. It offered a huge area for military assembly and drill, government proclamations, games, fiestas, even bullfights. Local crowds often gathered there at the end of the Santa Fe Trail to buy eastern merchandise and to get news. Trail riders celebrated their arrival by gambling in the many bars.

Over the years the adobe Palace of the Governors was difficult to maintain, as its thick earth roof became a roof garden, with water trickling down inside during rainstorms. Finally in 1909 the United States Legislature made it into the Museum of New Mexico and appropriated funds for its restoration.

The area under the long front portal—the entire north side of the Plaza—became an open-air part of the museum, designated as proprietary area for Pueblo Indians to market their arts and crafts. Ever since, the Indian market there has been a major tourist attraction since visitors can see a wide range of Pueblo art as well as a colorful part of our early history. In addition, every August the largest Indian arts and crafts market in the world takes place around the Plaza and is attended by thousands of people from many countries.

Another aspect of Santa Fe history is reflected by the Romanesque St. Francis Cathedral, which stands out among the surrounding adobe buildings. Ironically, Frenchman Bishop Jean Baptiste Lamy, whose bronze statue stands in front of the building, constructed it and played a major role in shaping the fortunes of his Spanish colonial town.

Willa Cather, in her well-known *Death Comes for the Archbishop*, tells how after coming to the wild frontier town in 1851, Lamy restored clerical influence, established schools and a hospital, and brought to Santa Fe a climate of refinement. In 1869, Archbishop Lamy made a lasting statement by replacing the original simple adobe church with a cathedral to express God's glory in the style of his native France.

The next section of the brochure, subtitled "Around Santa Fe, the Most Interesting 50-mile Square in America, in the Heart of the Land of Enchantment," described the neighborhood, after mentioning the Cross of the Martyrs on the crest of a hill in the northern part of the city erected after the reconquest of Santa Fe in memory of the twenty-one friars who were murdered by the Indians during the 1680 Pueblo Revolt, and the Bishop's Chapel behind Bishop's Lodge north of Santa Fe. The third section was about the Indian pueblos, explaining that the Tewa Indians were peaceful farming and home-building people. I was fascinated to learn that the word *pueblo* we use for both their villages and them as a people, means "small village" in Spanish and was given to them by Francisco Vásquez de Coronado. The brochure said:

> On your trip to Santa Fe you should plan to visit one or more of the thirteen pueblos located up and down the Rio Grande River. In these picturesque settlements you will see their homes, ranging from flat, one-story adobe dwellings to the five-story apartment type structure at Taos with outside entrances reached by a series of ladders. You'll see their kivas (ceremonial chambers) and the Indian himself at the daily tasks in the fields, baking bread at outdoor adobe ovens, making pottery, or the children at their play. Each pueblo has its peculiar customs of dress and language; and, if you are fortunate enough to be there on their various feast days during the year, you may see them celebrate with their colorful and ancient ceremonial dances.

When people asked about visiting the pueblos, we would tell them that some might ask a fee for taking pictures, and always to remember that they were visitors and not to enter any buildings without invitation.

Later, I learned more about individual pueblos as I visited them. At Tesuque Pueblo, only eight miles north of Santa Fe

The author's first view of the Santa Fe Plaza at the "End of the Trail."

The Bacas' house at 909 Canyon Road—the author's first adobe home.

YO

ITS SERVICES:

- **TOURISTS.** Thousands of tourists throughout the year visit the Chamber office seeking accommodations, information on points of interest, things to do, historical data, road information, and many other subjects. Every possible effort is made to provide information desired; maps and literature are supplied.

- **NEW BUSINESS.** Hundreds of letters are answered and conferences held with persons coming here, who seek information regarding business opportunities and wish to make their home in Santa Fe. Statistical information is given insofar as possible and con-

- **COMMUNITY HOST.** Throughout each year Congressional representatives, nationally and internationally-known personalities, and dozens of groups of school children come to Santa Fe for business or pleasure. The Chamber of Commerce is often the community host to these people and assists in making arrangements for their many needs.

- **CONVENTIONS.** Letters are sent out almost every week to various groups inviting them to select Santa Fe as the site for their convention during the following year. In addi-

An article the author wrote for the *New Mexican* describing the objectives of the Chamber of Commerce.

HAMBER OF COMMERCE

makes

SANTA FE

its

business

eon club" . . . the Santa Fe Chamber of Commerce. Here is a civic organization
cers and members have made our 30,000 residents and 1,043 business organi-
ull time job. The Chamber's prime, long run objective, of course, is to aid by
ible means, the growth and prosperity of our city. In order to accomplish this
rganization acts as our representative in trying to attract tourists to Santa Fe,
ng information to hundreds of families who are prospective new residents and by
new businesses on the advisability of engaging in activities in Santa Fe. In addi-
Chamber of Commerce takes an active part in such civic functions as aiding in
ojects, seeking the improvement of existing community and civic facilities, wel-
portant delegations and visitors and constantly trying to find ways to make this

Chamber of Commerce staff. Left to right: Ned Gold, Babs Wiswall, Ann Baumann, Violet Kochendoerfer, and Jim Riley.

The Chamber of Commerce on Shelby Street just off the Plaza accross from La Fonda.Hotel.

THIS IS *Santa Fé*

FOR THE VISITOR

The Palace of the Governors, in Santa Fé, New Mexico, built in 1610, now is state...

THE ANCIENT CITY

Santa Fé (*La Villa Real de la Santa Fé de S...* cisco de Asis*) was founded in 1610 by Don... Peralta, governor of New Spain, during the rei... Charles II of Spain. One or more Indian pu... on the site in prehistoric times, Spanish co... Mexico came to the area in 1598, twenty-two... the Pilgrims landed at Plymouth Rock. No... Indians revolted in the year 1680 and occu... until 1692 when General Don Diego de V... an agreement with the Indians and the c... without bloodshed.

Mexico, which at the time included N... itself from Spain in 1821 and Santa... northern capitol under the Mexican... during the Mexican War, the United... session of the city. At the outbreak o... the States, the Southern Army of t... invaded the territory and for a brief... and Confederate flags were flown o... Union forces won a decided victor... Pass and re-occupied the city. Fo... settlement of New Mexico continu... hood was granted. The City of t... the capital and is the oldest ca... States. Through it all, the distin... phere of Santa Fe has changed...

Issued by the Santa Fe Ch...

THIS IS *Santa Fé*

FOR THE NEW RESIDENT

The Palace of the Governors, in Santa Fé, New Mexico, built in 1610, now is state museum.

THE ANCIENT CITY

Santa Fé (*La Villa Real de la Santa Fé de San Fran-cisco de Asis*) was founded in 1610 by Don Pedro de Peralta, governor of New Spain, during the reign of King Charles II of Spain. One or more Indian pueblos stood on the site in prehistoric times, Spanish colonists from Mexico came to the area in 1598, twenty-two years before the Pilgrims landed at Plymouth Rock. Northern Pueblo Indians revolted in the year 1680 and occupied Santa Fé until 1692 when General Don Diego de Vargas reached an agreement with the Indians and the city was re-taken without bloodshed.

Mexico, which at the time included New Mexico, freed itself from Spain in 1821 and Santa Fé remained the northern capitol under the Mexican regime. In 1846, during the Mexican War, the United States took pos-session of the city. At the outbreak of the War Between the States, the Southern Army of the Texas Volunteers invaded the territory and for a brief time both the Texas and Confederate flags were flown over Santa Fé. Later, Union forces won a decided victory at nearby Glorieta Pass and re-occupied the city. Following the war, the settlement of New Mexico continued, and in 1912, state-hood was granted. The City of the Holy Faith remained the capital and is the oldest capital city in the United States. Through it all, the distinctive charm and atmos-phere of Santa Fe has changed but little.

Part of a series of brochures the author wrote while office manager of the Chamber of Commerce.

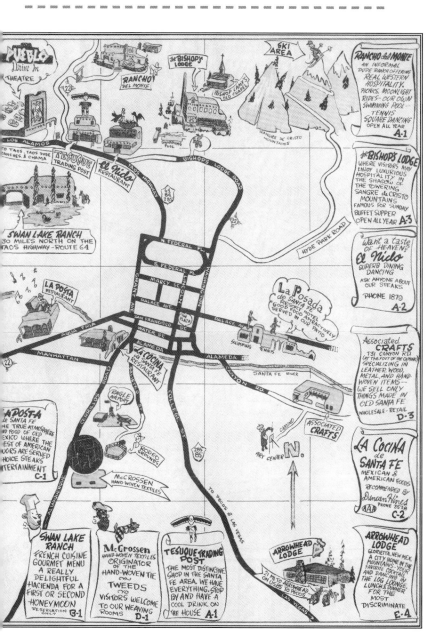

Front and back of tourist map of Santa Fe by cartoonist Ogilvie dated 1950.

Las Trampas Church before restoration and the addition of belfrys.

Altar screen at Las Trampas Church.

members worked farms and produced crafts. San Ildefonso Pueblo, twenty-two miles northwest, was one of the best-known pueblos of the Southwest—the home of famed potter Maria Martinez and her son Popovi Da. There the adobe houses faced two plazas, and in the center of one was an impressive ceremonial kiva. Santa Clara Pueblo was a sprawling colorful community twenty-seven miles northwest of Santa Fe, and attracted both casual visitors and the students of Indian lore.

San Juan Pueblo, located twenty-eight miles northwest of Santa Fe, was where the Spanish established the first capital of New Mexico in 1598. The Kramer Mercantile Company store was founded as a trading post for Indians and white settlers shortly after the Civil War. For many years the merchandise was imported from Missouri, brought in by wagon train.

Cochiti Pueblo, thirty miles southeast of Santa Fe, was known for excellent pottery and silver jewelry, while Nambe Pueblo, twenty miles northeast, was one of the smallest pueblos. Santo Domingo Pueblo, thirty-one miles southwest, was famous for its turquoise jewelry, excellent pottery, and weaving. In their elaborate Corn Dance held annually on August 4 and other ceremonies, Indians at Santo Domingo followed the customs and traditions of their forefathers more strictly than at any other pueblo.

San Felipe Pueblo, thirty-four miles south of Santa Fe, combined farming and production of handicrafts with notable success. Founded long before the arrival of the Spanish in 1540, San Felipe was one of the oldest settlements along the Rio Grande. Finally, Taos Pueblo, three miles outside Taos, was perhaps the most famous pueblo in the Southwest. Two communal houses, four and five stories high, faced each other across a large central plaza through which Taos Creek flowed. In addition to farming and raising stock, the Taos Indians were painters, bead workers, and drum makers. The pueblo was also noted for fine dancers and impressive ceremonials. An unforgettable image from my first visit was a Taos Indian standing on the roof of a small adobe building with arms across his chest, head lifted to the sun, and eyes closed. I was to learn that the intricate religion of the Pueblo Indians has much to offer our modern society.

The brochure *This Is Santa Fe for the Visitor* also described the nearby Indian ruins, including the ancient Indian cliff dwellings at Bandelier National Monument forty-five miles northwest of Santa Fe in Frijoles Canyon, where visitors could see ruins of old Indian villages dating from AD 1230, and the Puye Cliff Dwellings forty miles northwest, where Indians had lived long before white men had set foot on this continent.

Next, it depicted the native mountain villages which seemed an anachronism in modern times, and which I felt could connect tourists to New Mexican history as the villages had so dramatically done for me. I wanted to introduce visitors to the Penitente religious sect that had built small chapels called *moradas* and practiced distinctive religious rites during Lent.

I was told that during Holy Week Penitentes would crawl on hands and bare knees up to hilltop crosses, scourging their bare backs with yucca-bough whips. This was a practice brought from Spain by the Franciscan brothers, as I explained in the brochure:

> These practices persisted during Holy Week in the northernmost fringe of the Spanish Empire in the New World. This isolation in the 1800s was further emphasized shortly after the Mexican Revolution, when the Spanish-born Franciscans were expelled from the country and the native people were left to perform their own rituals—weddings, christenings, and funerals—the beginning of the lay Third Order of St. Francis.

Whenever I drove through these mountain villages of northern New Mexico or heard stories about the Penitentes, I always had a sense of the timelessness of ritual and the ancient history of my new home. And the fact that I and many other people had not learned about this history in school prompted me to write about the northern villages in the pamphlet. Traveling north from Santa Fe, the first village was Santa Cruz (Holy Cross), which was settled by colonists who came with Juan de Oñate in 1598 but was abandoned by the Spanish during the

Pueblo Revolt of 1680. After De Vargas ordered evacuation by the Indians in 1692, Santa Cruz, the second *villa royal* (Santa Fe being the first) was established.

For over three hundred years, Santa Cruz was on the main road between Santa Fe and Taos. The village church was one of the largest in New Mexico, and noteworthy because of its outstanding collection of fine old Spanish and Mexican paintings, together with rare books, letters and documents, parish registers, and church ornaments.

Chimayo, the next village in the charming and fertile Santa Cruz Valley, seemed timeless and was nationally known for its hand-woven rugs, blankets, and fabrics. In the 1950s, the people of Chimayo were proud but gracious to visitors and loved to demonstrate how their weaving was done by hand, emphasizing the patience and skill involved in creating each piece. In all the northern villages, crafts and traditions seemed to be honored.

Two miles south of Chimayo was El Santuario, a sacred shrine to which devout Catholics have made pilgrimages for hundreds of years. According to legend, Indians considered the site a sacred place centuries before the Spaniards arrived. The quaint adobe chapel with its twin towers topped with crosses and ancient weathered wooden gates—all within a walled patio—was a favorite subject for artists.

I attended a service there and was once again struck by the vivid colors of the altar's figures and decoration. After the service I was taken through a low door to the left of the altar, along a hallway with religious figures to a little room with a shallow well in the floor. There pilgrims have come for centuries to take samples of dirt, which is believed to have curative powers.

A privately owned square adobe about fifty feet from the Santuario contained a small statue of the Santo Niño Perdid—the Lost Child. The custodian there would respond to the ringing of the bells in the *campanile,* a separate bell tower as often seen in Europe. He sold layettes blessed by the Santo Niño to expectant mothers. Reportedly, these images of the Santo Niño would go out during the night on errands of mercy to the poor, and thus it was necessary to buy new shoes for the

Santo Niño every six months. Consequently, many offerings consisted of doll-sized shoes.

The next village traveling north was Cordova, where friends and I had once spent an unforgettable day with the Penitentes. Their large cross and *morada* were located at the upper end of town. I learned that for generations the residents of Cordova had specialized in wood carving of furniture, chests, trinkets, and *santos* (religious images). Perhaps the most famous Cordova carver was José Maria Lopez, who lived there until his death.

Proceeding through the hills, the small native village of Truchas was next. Here you entered narrow streets along a double row of adobe houses that lined a windy cliff edge overlooking Truchas Peak, which rises to 13,066 feet—the second highest peak in the state. Many houses had handsome handcarved wooden doors. Truchas had two small churches—one Catholic and one Presbyterian.

Further north in the direction of Taos was Las Trampas, the adobe walled town with a charming Spanish colonial church. Here, customs went back to Spanish colonial days, with crops harvested by hand and horses or goats used to trample out the grain.

Finally, four miles south of Taos was Ranchos de Taos, the small farming community best known for its massive adobe church, considered the most beautiful Spanish church in the Southwest. An impression of magnificence lingers long after visiting the large twin belfries topped with crosses, the great doors with unusual fan-like decoration, the huge buttresses, and the hallowed *camposanto* (cemetery), the resting place for the dead—all enclosed by plastered adobe walls six feet high. The church was erected in 1779 during the period when Father Serra Junipero was establishing many of California's earliest missions.

After slowly driving through the northern hills, stopping at these little Spanish villages, each with a story to tell, joining the fast highway traffic into Taos was like coming back to another world.

The Chamber of Commerce brochure for tourists entitled *What to Do in Santa Fe* described the numerous activities and celebrations in the City Different and surrounding area. At the pueblos, Indians celebrated their feast days different times of the year with sacred dances—in summer for rain and growth, in winter for abundant game and success in hunting. These included the Buffalo Dance, Eagle Dance, Green Corn Dance, Deer Dance, and special ones at Fiesta and Christmas. I also reminded visitors that if they came over Labor Day weekend they would experience Fiesta de Santa Fe, the oldest community celebration in America. Fiesta de Santa Fe began in 1712 to commemorate De Vargas's bloodless reconquest of Santa Fe from the Indians. Friday evening celebrations began with the burning of Zozobra (Old Man Gloom) and ended four event-filled days later in a gay swirl of street dancing under the stars.

In the brochure I also described Aspen Week, usually in early October when the high mountain country was ablaze with golden color and many activities took place, including golf, square dancing, summer theater, rodeos, and riding. There was also fishing and hunting by horseback or by jeep or plane for bear, elk, deer, antelope, wild turkey, prairie chicken, quail, grouse, pheasant, duck, geese, coot, band-tailed pigeon, snipe, rails, and gallinules. Overall, the brochure emphasized the diversity of activities available in or around the City Different.

The brochure *This is Santa Fe for the New Resident* included fascinating information about society and education in the 1950s. It first described the local schools, which, in addition to the public grade and high schools and several private schools, included Catholic boarding schools for men and women at the high school and college level.

I mentioned the excellent daily newspaper, the *Santa Fe New Mexican,* which was located at 202 East Marcy Street and had an annual subscription fee of $10.00 a year, $6.00 for six months, and $1.25 for one month.

At that time there were two radio stations, KVSP (CBS affiliate) and KTRC (ABC affiliate) but no FM broadcasts. Today, it's almost unbelievable to me that at the time I said, "Although there are a few television sets, with reception via Albuquerque, this has not proved too successful as yet." We listened instead to the radio for news and entertainment. Free of the overload of commercial tube, we would have been unbelieving had someone predicted the coming of the Internet.

We used natural gas for heating and refrigeration. Although there was sufficient water in the city for ordinary use, private wells were required for property outside the city limits. And due to water scarcity, all gardening and agriculture had to be done using irrigation. With rainfall undependable, and before technology of deep wells and running water, *acequias* carrying runoff from the mountains were an essential part of the town's life. An elaborate system of irrigation law provided rights of ownership supervised by the *majordomo de la acequias* (supervisor of irrigation ditches). There was an important annual celebration of the cleaning of the ditches. Today, Acequia madra (mother ditch), which runs along the street that bears its name, is the only ditch that remains from the early days.

In the brochure *This Is Santa Fe for New Business,* I noted that because Santa Fe did not have heavy industry and many local residents had outside incomes, the city had never been affected much by either recessions or periods of prosperity, and that Santa Fe's growth had accelerated during the post-World War II period without any boom. Normally fluctuation in national business trends were not felt in Santa Fe for six months to a year after beginning in the East; and as a result the country's recession that began in early 1948 had not been noticeable in Santa Fe.

As to business opportunities, I suggested that the fact that the number of business licenses had tripled since 1942 was primarily due to the presence of the Atomic Energy Commission and people living at Los Alamos, who did most of their shopping in Santa Fe. As a result, we had more businesses than a community of Santa Fe's size could normally support. I included the information that there was a 2 percent sales tax on most purchases and that state income tax was 1 percent on the first $10,000 taxable income, 2 percent on the second $10,000, with 3 percent on the next $80,000.

In light of the current skyrocketing Santa Fe property values, this is what I said in my brochure forty-five years ago:

Rental property. Due to the heavy influx of summer

tourists, rental properties are scarce until after mid-September, with rents comparatively high. There is some turnover; but it is necessary for one to be here to take advantage of vacancies as they occur. In all probability, it may take some time before suitable housing can be found. The Chamber office maintains listings of houses and apartments for use of new residents.

There is no YMCA or YWCA in Santa Fe. However, the Chamber of Commerce maintains a listing of rooms in private homes for those wishing this type of accommodation. Often it is advisable for new residents to rent until they can find suitable permanent housing.

Property for Purchase. In addition to the usual turnover in property, there are several housing developments being constructed under the GI and FHA finance plans, and such housing in the low-cost fields will be available during 1950 and 1951.

In the section "Building in Santa Fe," I explained our zoning laws and described our traditional adobe and Territorial styles. Then I said that land and property values had always been stable in Santa Fe—that prices and valuation were considerably higher then than they had been prior to the war, which was in keeping with the national trend. I added that there had been no property boom in Santa Fe, but neither had there been a recession of property values—that prices had been substantially maintained, which showed that residential property values were sound. Property taxes on both real and residential property for 1948 were $26.96 per thousand assessed valuation, which was at the rate of approximately 30 percent of full value.

Under "General Information," I shared facts on location, altitude, and climate, describing health benefits for certain maladies due to the clear, high, dry climate. I mentioned that our population was made up of 95.3 percent native white (many of Spanish descent), 2 percent foreign-born white, .7 percent black, and 2 percent Indian.

Under "Cost of Living," I noted that prices in Santa Fe were not low. Because all food and merchandise were shipped from outside the state, many items purchased were slightly more expensive than in areas which are nearer their source of supply. I added, however, that the informality of life in Santa Fe was such that expenditures normally essential in other cities were not required; and the average resident lived as inexpensively as in other southwestern cities.

In writing these brochures with the help of library personnel, businessmen, members of the Chamber of Commerce, and longtime residents, I gained knowledge and even greater respect for the people, culture, and history of my new home. I had educated myself to the point where I felt right at home and even more proud to be a part of it all.

During this time the many projects I was involved in while working for the Chamber of Commerce brought me into contact with more and more aspects of northern New Mexico society and culture. Before I arrived in Santa Fe, one of the big projects at the Chamber of Commerce focused on the Santa Fe Ski Basin. Before going to Santa Fe, the idea that there might be skiing in what I considered desert country would have been something amusing. But later I became deeply involved with skiing in New Mexico and Colorado. With a limited budget, Sierras de Santa Fe, Inc., built tiny Sierra Ski Lodge and a 2,600-foot double chairlift made from bucket seats of C-47s welded together. The lift started at an elevation of l0,300 and went up a half-mile.

Located seventeen miles from Santa Fe up a scenic mountain road, the new Ski Basin was strategically nestled in the Sangre de Cristo Mountains. The road up was narrow, curvy, snow-covered, and often precarious, even after ancient plows had cleared it. I can still see the driver of a VW bug stewing as the road wasn't wide enough for him to pass the bigger cars which could not move. During a recent visit, I was impressed with how much safer conditions are today. The road has been widened, and there is roadside parking way down from the lodge, where skiers can leave their cars and be shuttled to the top.

The first lodge was a mere shack by today's standards, with restroom, seating to eat or warm up, and a few benches outside on a wooden platform overlooking the chairlift. But the lodge

-- -- -- -- -- -- -- -- -- -- -- -- -- -- -- -- -- -- -- --

was beloved by the locals. Sierras de Santa Fe developers hoped it would attract skiers from around the country. That would be our job at the Chamber of Commerce.

Running the Ski Basin was sometimes a headache that first year—like when I would get word that the water pipes were frozen again! The pipes had not been installed deep enough; and I was instructed to hire men to buy coal, dig out spots under the pipes, and build little fires to thaw the line. This was a questionable arrangement, for when water started flowing, sometimes toilets or the kitchen sink at the lodge would overflow. However, by the next year things were under control, and our brochure said:

SKI ON THE TOP OF THE WORLD
Out West Where the Skiing Is Best.

Enthusiastic skiers are traveling West for deep powder snow, vast open slopes and brilliant sunshine. American skiing at its best is found in the Rocky Mountains, and the West's newest development is the Santa Fe Basin.

We made a "Fun for Everyone" dedication plan for a big two-day open house on February 4 and 5 of 1950, promising "racing, exhibition skiing, ice skating, free coffee, doughnuts and soft drinks, and free rides on the lift as time will allow." At the opening ceremonies, a special trail was named for Charles LeFeber, a longtime supporter who had seen his dream fulfilled.

Situated as it was, the open slopes from the top of the chairlift were admirably suited to the average skier, while veteran skiers could find more rugged terrain by going up higher than the power lift terminal. To encourage beginners and children, there was also a rope-tow area. And the powder snow at that altitude ensured good skiing from early fall to late spring.

The Ski Basin was very popular with crowds coming from Los Alamos, Albuquerque, Las Vegas, and even Texas; and we at the Chamber of Commerce made plans to tap the Midwest with ski trains from Chicago, Kansas City, and towns along the Santa Fe Railway, plus air excursions with special flights on TWA, Pioneer, and Continental Airlines. In advertising, we even targeted eager New Englanders.

When a ski meet had to be postponed at Lake Placid because of scanty snow, we sent a wire inviting them to Santa Fe, explaining that the dry desert air gave us powdery snow from early November until late April; and the rapid evaporation in the thin atmosphere of our Southwest's towering peaks made for snow conditions unexcelled on American ski slopes.

The manager of the Ski Basin was Ernie Blake, who had an interesting background to go with his foreign accent. His extensive knowledge of skiing began at age four in Europe at St. Moritz. Born of Swiss parents in Germany, he was sent to school in Switzerland, where skiing was part of the curriculum. Hockey was Ernie's love during his college days in France and Germany, where he became familiar with the top resorts of Europe. His family then sent him to England to learn banking and English. When the family later moved to America, his first job at Saks Fifth Avenue interested him in representing Lanz ski clothing. Promotion then took him to the West, where he discovered western alpine resorts.

During World War II, he was attached to British Intelligence because of his knowledge of languages. Since this position required him to assume an Anglo-Saxon name, that's when he became Ernest Blake. Later in the Third Army under Patton, he helped to interrogate high German commanders. Then after the war his business travel took him to Santa Fe, where he learned of the proposed ski development and decided to invest in the venture. Because of his enviable skiing knowledge and experience, he became manager, and under his leadership the basin grew and prospered.

Years later, after the Santa Fe Ski Basin had become well known, Ernie moved to the Taos area, where he built an upscale resort noted for its steep trails. One evening I was amused in watching a late TV show featuring ski lodges around the country and saw Ernie's Taos run featured with a special emphasis on his martini trees. Supposedly, atop some of the steep runs skiers could find a jug of martinis strapped to a tree. The rationale was that relaxation resulted in better skiing, and martinis are known to work fast.

CHAPTER 3

INITIATION TO NORTHERN NEW MEXICO CULTURE

In writing about the Spanish villages for Chamber of Commerce brochures, I recalled a trip I took with Audrey and Al on the High Road to Taos, where the people of Las Trampas had shown us their classic adobe church with *santos*. Their bright colors standing out like shining lights against the brown adobe remained in my memory. On that excursion Al had called Las Trampas a prize example of Spanish colonial architecture and remarked that this was "Penitente country." I didn't know at the time what he meant, but I was to find out.

That year during Holy Week I was invited to join two friends to experience what we could of this Penitente ritual. Dave and John were two Yalies who had come to Santa Fe and opened The Centerline—an adobe front shop on Marcy Street one block down Washington Street from the Plaza. A big sidewalk window displayed Swedish modern furniture and other lovely furnishings, as well as artwork they had collected on trips to foreign countries.

On Good Friday we took the afternoon off and drove to Cordova. We had seen Penitente *moradas* with only one tiny window high in the wall, in which outsiders were never allowed, and had heard of the frenzied religious rites in the small dark buildings during which participants sometimes had been trampled to death.

Toward evening we saw people leaving the Cordova *morada* headed toward the local adobe Catholic church. Even though we seemed to be the only Anglos, we felt part of the crowd and ended up under the high-vaulted ceiling of the church, where we sat down in a pew toward the back.

From there, in the dim light we watched a procession enter

the church headed by the *hermano mayor* (chief brother) of the Lay Order of St. Francis. He carried in his arms a life-sized statue of the crucified, bleeding Christ. Beside him walked the cloaked *rezador* (man of prayer), chanting the ritual from a small book; and on his other side was the *pitero,* whose wooden *pito* (flute) produced a shrill, ear-piercing sound. They were followed by five cross bearers, each with a *companero* (partner) on either side. Then came the initiates, with rolled-up jeans, moving up the center aisle on bare knees, their bare backs scarred and bloody from flagellation with yucca boughs.

Behind the long table at the altar, were no Catholic priests in robes but ordinary lay Spanish in plain clothes, including one in a plaid wool jacket. As the sun set, the windowless church grew dark, and a twelve-candle candelabra on the altar became the only light. We no longer could see what was going on around us and could only listen, though we could not understand the Spanish.

After some kind of liturgy and the clackety clack of large *metracas,* the candles, which had something to do with the Twelve Disciples, were extinguished one by one until the huge church was in utter darkness. It was eerie being the only three Anglos surrounded by hundreds of emotionally charged Spanish. Then, following a long wondering silence, we heard the clanking of heavy chains accompanying the reading of the individual names of those who had died that past year. After what seemed ages, we emerged from the church into a starry New Mexico night, feeling strangely chastened and in awe of the deep commitment of these Penitentes, who lived in another world.

Shortly after coming to Santa Fe Audrey had introduced me to John Sauk, who encouraged my interest in Santa Fe square dancing groups. I wrote family and friends:

January 30, 1950

The square dance class turned out to be great fun, with sessions from 8 to 11:45. If you've ever tried it, you know what a workout it can be. Instead of learning a few squares as I expected, we were dancing schottisches, the varsouvianna (a Spanish dance), polkas, waltzes, etc.

"We" was another couple and John and I, who were invited to the Chavezes afterward. Stella Chavez works at W. C. Krugers—Audrey's architectural office—and though it's pronounced "Ha-zooz" with a long *a*, her husband's name is spelled Jesus, which always throws me when I see it in print. Stella's a great gal, attractive, with wavy black hair and sparkly black eyes. She brought out the Scotch, which soothed our dry throats before coffee. We talked till after two.

Got to bed by three and worked Saturday morning with Babs Wiswall at the Chamber. We'd just hired her to do the student mailing. She picked me up after lunch, and we headed for San Juan Pueblo to see the Indian Basket Dance. I'd heard so much about these ceremonials at the pueblos. This was my first. I loved the adobe houses, often built with common walls like apartments. Each pueblo seems to have two clans, one living on one side of the plaza and the other across from them.

They dress in costume most of the time, with their bright shawls. The men have individual ways of doing their hair. Some have long braids, with a special way of braiding in bright ribbons or felt. The kids are adorable—they're different and lovable like puppies!

The Tewa Indians in the pueblos around here are fairly prosperous and quite independent, but deeply religious. Now and then you see one silently standing with eyes closed, undoubtedly in silent meditation or prayer. In their underground ceremonial chambers they call their kivas, the men commune with the Great Spirit. Only men go down on ladders stuck through a hole in the flat roof of big round buildings. Women and even children some-times join the men in some ceremonial dances outside, praying for crops and things. I hear, though, that elders worry about young Indians, who seem less interested in the historic customs.

Could sleep longer on Sunday. Babs wanted to go to the

Buffalo Dance at San Ildefonso Pueblo. Marcel dela Harpe, a friend of hers, was to have taken us in his station wagon but seems he had a dinner engagement. So it was decided we'd call his host and tell him Marcel was bringing a guest. Then I'd be an excuse for us to leave early and go to San Ildefonso.

I went to dinner with Marcel and his cousin. Marcel is a Russian who has a guest ranch just out of Santa Fe. His cousin Falker is a tall, blue-eyed blonde who recently arrived in the U.S. Seems he started out from Estonia with an older fellow with plans to cross the Atlantic to America on some sort of raft arrangement. Luckily, they were picked up by a freighter about 400 miles off the coast of Ireland and brought to Ellis Island. He speaks good English, German, and French. Marcel does, too.

We drove out to San Sebastian (a country community of artists about fifteen miles out of Santa Fe) to the home of host Helmuth Naumer, a German artist. As I was introduced, I found I knew Mrs. Naumer, who is the Home Service secretary at the local Red Cross chapter. Their home is typically Santa Fe style with corner kiva fireplaces and such.

Another guest was an old character by the name of Taylor, who had really led a colorful life as a bandit in Mexico during the Revolution—actually fought with Pancho Villa, the king of the bandits! He spun some yarns you wouldn't believe happened on our continent. The history of this country is an eye-opener to me, which almost puts the old New England stories to shame, time-wise at least!

During drinks and a savory chicken dinner, I learned about artist Naumer himself. He's a quiet, soft-spoken middle-aged chap, whose presence belies the fact that he's a top-flight rider. When he's off, he doesn't follow highways or trails, but takes a straight course no matter what's ahead—mountains, canyons, streams. Marcel said on one trip in following Helmuth, his trousers were all but torn from his legs.

Our plan worked! We left after eight, picked up Babs,

and headed for the Buffalo Dance at San Ildefonso. On the way I thought of all the different countries represented there that evening. With our own Spanish, Anglo, and Indian cultures, Santa Fe seems a gathering place for many others, and not only artists!

The Buffalo Dance was exciting. All over the pueblo, on the ground and even on the tops of some of the adobe buildings, were bright *luminarias* (little bonfires of pungent smelling piñon pine). They're there partly for warmth but mostly for light, as the hunters come in from the hills to the pueblo plaza, each man with a head of antlers. They lean sharply forward on two short sticks to simulate a four-legged animal. Side-by-side they formed two lines facing each other. Then, after a few moments they all faced out and then turned in, and did this over and over again. Some little boys were antelopes, too! The Indians seem to have a special kind of symbolic love of animals!

After a long dance, with their special kind of stomping and chanting, and the tom-tom of the drums, the hunters took off for the mountains and the hunt, to return in the morning. We drove back to Santa Fe, had some hot stuff at Babs's, got to bed about 12:30. Up again at 4:30, we drove back to see the hunters come in. It was quite a weekend.

Square danced again this past week, and on the weekend went skiing up at the basin with Babs and some of her friends from Los Alamos. It snowed all day, but skiing was perfect with our wonderful powder snow. Have you noticed that the international skiers have been sitting around Lake Placid waiting for snow so they could have their meet? Well, we at the chamber sent them a wire describing our beautiful powder snow and inviting them to bring the meet to Santa Fe Basin!

Jim Riley lets us use the chamber season lift ticket, so we save a little money. Oh yes, I was invited to the Rileys for dinner a couple of weeks ago. I learned that Jim had been a chaplain overseas during the war, and his wife Rhoda was with him. We had a wonderful evening swapping sto-

ries about the war. They're grand people and live just out
of Santa Fe in an adobe they built themselves. It is spacious and rambling because they keep adding rooms as
they're needed.

Rhoda's quite an artist and has decorated walls in the
kids' rooms, and painted some of the glass windows with
the quaint Santa Fe designs. I have an invitation to drop
in anytime. So you see I'm not sitting here twittering my
thumbs!

I gained more knowledge of local construction techniques
one day when the Rileys, who were building an addition to
their house, invited me to learn how to make adobes. I drove
out and joined Jim at a big flat spot behind their house. As he
started digging a big hole in the ground, he explained that it
had to be the right kind of earth without excessive clay (which
shrinks in drying) or too much sand (which gives it a tendency
to crumble). Then he poured in water, added some straw, and
mixed everything together before shoveling it into wooden
molds on the ground.

Jim noted that the molds were about four inches thick,
divided to make four bricks about ten inches wide and fourteen
inches long. Forms had handles on the sides so they could be
lifted off to make more bricks and allow air to circulate for
quicker drying.When the bricks are dry after several days, they
can be used like regular bricks in building thick walls with
adobe plaster in between.

Jim mentioned that typical Santa Fe style adobe buildings
were rarely more than one story high. At window height, the
window frame is installed and adobes built around it. At ceiling height, *vigas* (long, thin logs, like telephone poles) are laid
across between the side walls. The walls are then built a bit
higher around the logs, and you see the *vigas* sticking through
on the outside. Then wood strips are laid across the *vigas* inside
to support more adobe as a roof. Sometimes these cross boards
are installed in a beautiful design. Of course, the *vigas* are part
of the interior ceiling decor, sometimes with carved decorative

corbels at the supporting walls. The roofs of some old adobes are green with growing plants.

I'd always wondered how Indians or early settlers were able to raise the heavy *vigas* and secure them in place until I saw an illustration. One end of two or more strong poles is anchored on the ground with the other end lifted up to the roof level at an angle to form a track. Then the *vigas* are rolled up.

I mentioned that Jim had added straw to the wet mixture to strengthen adobe bricks; and walls are plastered with adobe mud after chicken wire has been attached so the mud will hold more securely. Many years later old buildings may have to be replastered, though some old adobes are charming after weather has produced intricate waterway artistry. The lessons about building I received from the Rileys gave me a much greater appreciation for local craftsmanship and the intimate connection between the area's architecture and the land.

A few Sundays later was to have been a big ski weekend; but it had started snowing Friday night and was still going strong on Sunday. The road up would be impassible. In the morning I wrote a long letter home and spent the afternoon and evening at Audrey and Al's listening to good music, playing canasta, and sharing a supper of Al's enchiladas. In my letter I said:

February 11, 1951

One day last week Babs said they needed more wood for their fireplace and were going out to Marcelle's Rancho La Barberia to get some. On the way out we talked about Falker, Marcel's Estonian cousin.

They said he was on Ellis Island for six months while Marcelle pulled strings. Then, with the help of local politicos, Falker and his friend were let in by act of Congress. In addition to English, German, and French, they both speak Russian. Falker looked quite German (the typical Hitler Aryan type) with blonde hair and blue eyes. He was noticeably polite compared to most Americans!

I'd heard that four men were living at Rancho La Barberia, and pictured a messy ramshackled place. Was I surprised! I couldn't believe what I saw! It's back in the mountains about fifteen miles from town in a setting which seems specially designed—a big bowl with mountains all around. Then there are the stables and two little guest houses that go with the big adobe ranch house high up on one side. Long, L-shaped wings stretch around, with portals (adobe open porches) and a large flagstone patio overlooking the valley.

La Barberia got its name from one small wing, which is very old. It had been a barber shop of what had been a tiny community at the end of the old Santa Fe Trail, where trail men used to stop and get slicked up before hitting the big town. Oh yes, there's also a tiny adobe chapel with a carved, weathered gate.

The long living room, with flagstone floor, has one friendly grouping of white leather upholstered furniture, and drapes of heavy white hand-woven wool. Then, two steps up toward the other end, there's a huge fireplace like one's always dreamed about. Built-in seats on one side are covered with white angora fur pillows, which you just sink into. In front of the fireplace are two dark blue corduroy mattresses about four by seven, covered with white wool rugs. You can stretch out full length and watch the fire. It's just perfect!

The master bedroom occupies one whole wing and is strictly Hollywood—mostly in white with a huge fireplace all across one end. The bed has a high white satin tufted headboard. Fluffy white rugs cover the flagstone floor in front of two white corduroy-covered studio couches on either side of a huge desk at the other end, with a window seat from which you look out over the valley.

Next to it is a room half as big as my house with sliding-door closets all around, from which you go up three steps into a huge bathroom with fancy plumbing fixtures, a big white circular fur rug in the center, with tufted stools around, etc. Then there's a kitchen and dining room with heavy antique table and chairs. I didn't ask who their housekeeper was, but I surely did wonder!

So much for the guest ranch. We transferred to the open jeep and took off on a road we couldn't see most of the time 'cause it was covered with snow. We headed cross country into the mountains. Falker could surely handle a jeep, and gave us a ride for our money. Sometimes there'd be a big hole covered with snow, and the jeep would practically tip over. He'd take off the road through the trees, cutting down steep banks to get back on the road. Only a jeep, sometimes in four-wheel drive low range, could have done it! After driving what seemed miles, we got near the top, where we found good fallen wood, and sat in the sun after loading the jeep.

Falker wanted me to drive back. I'd have loved to, but I knew I'd not have the nerve to drive fast enough and we'd get stuck. So we had another wild ride back, tea at the ranch, and came on into town. I had dinner with Babs, and Audrey and Al stopped by after their square dancing. Now some big news!

One day at work Jim Riley said, "Vi, I know a great gal who has an apartment in the first house on Canyon Road. Her roommate is leaving, and she's looking for a replacement. Would you like to meet her?" Well, I love my little house and had just gotten settled in; but I said I would. Jim called the woman, Mary Pollard, and we made a date to have a drink at La Fonda after work the next day.

I was pretty excited at the thought of living in the first house on Canyon Road, because it's so important here in Santa Fe—a spot every tourist is bound to pass as they go out to the little shops where artists sell their stuff, and they'll want to tell friends they had lunch at a historic eating place out there. After my experience the day I came to Santa Fe, I did some reading about it.

It truly is, as they say, one of the most historic and picturesque streets in the States—the oldest one still in use, believe it or not! The Pueblo Indians had it as a trail at least a century before any of we white folks arrived to stay. Today's Canyon Road follows that trail along the Santa Fe River that took them over the Sangre de Cristos to the

Pecos Pueblo. The Spanish conquistadors named it—they called it *El camino de canon*.

The Canyon Road we now know goes back to the early eighteenth century when the Spanish started cultivating the fields and building homes along that *camino*. Their houses were those great old adobes (some still standing) which actually set the pattern for our Santa Fe style that's not changed too much ever since. Many were built flush with the road. That's what gave me that funny feeling the day I first drove in—of being channeled through a long tunnel. And remember I said back then I wondered what was behind all those walls on either side of the unpaved road?

I now know that there are wonderful living spaces built around central patios, or placitas. Then, as Spanish families grew and children started their own families, they would add new rooms and even separate buildings. These rambling adobe compounds were wonderful centers for family and social life leading to neighborly community.

With a Canyon Road address, it would be hard to know where one family's property begins and where it ends. There are areas of grass and growing things in small personal patios, all blocked from the dust and noise of the road by big walls. It's the many shapes and sizes of buildings and properties, along with the family privacy, that makes Canyon Road unique and so special.

And now saying all this makes me excited about the prospects, and I hope all goes well tomorrow. If it does, I'll call you so you'll know before you get this letter!

I planned to call after meeting with Mary the next day. I wondered what she would be like.

CHAPTER 4

LIFE on CANYON ROAD
and TAOS TRADITIONS

When I went to meet my potential roommate Mary Pollard, Jim was at La Fonda to introduce us and buy us a drink before he left. Mary was an attractive brunette about my age, a bit taller than my five eight, and had soft brown eyes and a genial smile that made me relax immediately as she began telling me about her family.

They had lived in Taos before moving to Santa Fe, where her stepfather was on the Supreme Court. Her mother, who was from an old Virginia family, was always reminding her of social niceties. In Taos, the family had been good friends of the Pueblo Indians, some of whom had worked for them. In Santa Fe, Mary worked for the State Health Department and traveled a lot; so if we decided to live together, I'd have the apartment to myself a good deal—an attractive prospect.

After our talk, we stopped by to see the apartment just over the Santa Fe River bridge on the left side of Canyon Road. The big house at 202 Canyon Road was in the Territorial adobe style, with two guest houses in back and a large garden area from Canyon Road to the Santa Fe River.

The apartment, which had its own house number of 205, was a back half of the big house, with a private driveway from Canyon Road to an open porch, where double French doors led to the living room. There was an adobe kiva fireplace in one far corner of the living room alongside two large windows that looked out over Canyon Road. The large tub in the bathroom looked inviting after my tiny shower, and I also liked the kitchen, which had a little back porch, and the bedroom with its four large closets.

As we left, Mary said, "Vi, I can't say yes right now. I've a meeting tomorrow with another gal who's interested in sharing the apartment. After I meet with her, I'll call you."

The next day Mary called to tell me she wanted me to be her roommate, saying, "I had a weird experience with the other gal, Vi. She said she came to Santa Fe to do some writing and needs to find a job; but all the while she talked, her mind seemed to be far, far away—almost as though I weren't there. I know I don't want to live with her, so when can you move in?" I went home and called my family in Minnesota, telling them I now had an interesting roommate and a new home in the best area of Santa Fe.

Later, I learned why Mary had had a weird experience with the other woman who wanted to share the apartment. This woman had ended up renting the guest house I'd vacated, and kept calling to visit us at 205 Canyon Road. Although I put her off twice, telling her that Mary was out of town, and suggesting it would be best to come when we were both home, one evening there was a knock at the door. Before I opened it, I could see her through the French door, and her jeep in the driveway.

I let her in. Shortly after we started a conversation, she made me feel uncomfortable because of the personal questions she was asking, especially about Mary. I replied, "Mary's my roommate, but I'm not about to answer such personal questions." As a quiet hostility began to fill the air, she got up from her chair and walked toward me as I sat mesmerized. Looking down, she said, "Well, we don't seem to be able to establish any rapport" and started for the door.

I rose and followed her, saying apologetically, "I'm sorry. I might have offered you a drink or something." Then she turned and replied, "I have some good jazz records and a bottle of burgundy at the apartment. Would you like to come by?"

I will never know why I said yes, and was apprehensive as I went into the bedroom to put on some lipstick, saying to myself, "Vi, what are you getting yourself into?" However, it turned out to have been the best decision I could have made.

After listening to records and having some wine, she found out what she really wanted to know. I was not interested in a relationship. When I described the evening to Mary, she mentioned that in Santa Fe it was best to have your own apartment. Some people thought if two women were living together they were lesbians. I also learned that driving a jeep was labeling oneself.

I had grown up in Minnesota in the 1920s, in a sheltered region of the country, when our hearts could still be young and gay without question. Now I was learning that gays found art colonies places where they could live more openly than in general society. Some of Mary's friends in the State Health Department were lesbians, and became good friends. And later, I had another learning experience about gays.

Mary had several snapshots stuck in the edge of the mirror in our bedroom. One was of Terry, who belonged to a big Taos family and was traveling around the country recording folk songs. On one of our many trips to Taos, Mary took me to meet Joe and Margue Foster, a couple who knew Terry and lived at Ranchos de Taos in an ancient adobe that had weeds growing out of the roof. On the way Mary explained that Margue Foster had multiple sclerosis, and when friends came by Joe expected them to wait outside for a while so he could have time to get her situated in a living room chair. If one didn't know Margue couldn't walk, one would never have guessed.

When we entered the charming adobe on this occasion, I was entranced. We watched our step as floors were different levels—floors of an exquisite opaque white, glistening here and there as they provided a perfect background for old Navajo rugs. The furniture, which Joe had designed and built, was Spanish-modern and painted black, adding the perfect contrast to the floors. Three fireplaces hugged corner walls of the large living room.

As we sat down, I learned about the unusual construction of the house and was cautioned not to lean back in my chair because the legs might dig into the earthen floor! When I expressed amazement, Joe continued: "It's pretty fragile, Vi, and we keep it nice and white by mopping with watered tierra blanca—the white earth we get from the arroyo. The glitter is mica."

I then listened as Mary and the Fosters talked about Terry's family. They had all lived in Taos and watched Terry and his siblings grow up. Discussing Terry's family one by one, they remarked that each had done something special and unusual. Then Joe astonished me by saying, "But then, when you have a lesbian for a father. . . ."

At first I thought I had heard incorrectly. Later, I learned that Terry's mother had been a Shakespearean actress who, after divorce or the death of her husband, had invited a woman friend to move in with the family—a lesbian who had filled the father role. In later conversations Joe told me more about the gay community in the area, remarking that there was great jealousy in some instances because gay relationships were then more difficult to come by.

The Fosters later became good friends to whom I took other friends to meet since they could converse easily about any subject. Because they were housebound, they did a lot of reading. I'd noticed walls of books and coffee tables covered with magazines. Since they had lived three and a half years in Rome, Venice, Seville, Madrid, and Paris, they could always add a European perspective to the conversation. If I brought along an architect or physicist, we'd get deeply involved in discussions about their fields.

In addition, Joe was also a published author. One day we discussed his novel that had just been accepted, entitled *A Cow Is Too Much Trouble in Los Angeles*—the story of a Mexican family who moved to the big city. Joe's editor called it "the funniest, saddest book of the year. . . a pure delight to read." For me, the Fosters were another fascinating example of a creative couple who felt the Land of Enchantment a source of inspiration. I was to discover many more.

Through Mary I also had the opportunity to meet local

Indians, especially those of Taos Pueblo. Mary was known to all the Taos Indians, some of whom had worked for her family while they had lived in Taos. Because Pueblo Indians were usually quiet and reserved around Anglos, it was wonderful to watch them eagerly come up to Mary, throwing their arms around her and saying, "Mary, we've missed you!"

One year at the San Geronimo Festival at Taos Pueblo, Mary pointed out a handsome Indian, remarking: "That man over there, Vi, is Augustino." He was being unusually talkative to a couple of tourists, and we moved closer to listen. After the couple left, Mary walked over, shaking her finger at him, saying, "Augustino, what were you telling those people?" He grinned and replied, "They ask me questions. I give 'em answers. Now they go home and write a book!"

I listened to Augustino as Mary kept asking about mutual friends. Then, as we were leaving, Augustino said, "I sometimes go to Albuquerque to see relatives, and Santa Fe is on the way," indicating he might visit. Later, Mary advised me about Indian etiquette. "Indians are open, generous people, Vi. They will do anything for you; but they also expect you to do the same for them—like Augustino just might stop by your home with his whole family on the way to Albuquerque expecting to spend the night."

Then she said something more. "Never ask direct questions of Indians, Vi." Even though I didn't like the thought, I was glad Mary had told me this, for I continually wanted to ask questions about their customs and culture—about the statue-like figures I'd seen standing motionless against a high wall, or what went on in their kiva, a round flat-topped structure with a ladder sticking out from the center of the top. Time and again I had to remember Mary's admonition.

One Taos Pueblo couple I met through Mary became fast friends. In the winter, Emily and Eliseo Concha lived at the pueblo in what they called "our trailer house"—a long, narrow apartment on the third floor of the famous five-story Taos

Pueblo. Because most adobes are one-story buildings, the facade of Taos Pueblo is unique and impressive, with each floor divided into several living areas. To get to the Conchas' front door, I had first to climb one picturesque outdoor ladder first to a little platform, and then another. In the summer, Emily and Eliseo lived in a cottage with a garden on the banks of a stream some distance from the pueblo.

Eliseo was a handsome man, his long black hair braided with colorful felt. He taught manual arts at the Pueblo Indian School. Emily was short and chubby, with a shy grin that reflected her genial personality. I was entranced with their child-like qualities. The couple looked forward to our visits. One time they did not answer our knocks or our calls as Mary and I came to pick them up for a dance at Big Hull outside of Taos. Then, just as we were about to leave, they dashed out from around a corner, waving and laughing.

The hall for the celebration that night was an unusually large two-story barn-like adobe with inside walls covered in bright murals painted by Taos artists. Everyone was pleased and amused when Eliseo won the waltz contest. In handing him a $10.00 bill, the MC said, "We all go to the pueblo to see Eliseo do his own dances, and then he comes in and cops the prize at ours!" There was great applause, and to celebrate later we took Eliseo out to our car for a drink. By our law it was then illegal for Indians to buy or to possess liquor, which was typical of the many ways we treated them as inferior human beings.

Although the Conchas were generally glad to see us when we visited Taos Pueblo, one time was different. I was taking a friend new to Santa Fe on the regular Taos tour to meet my friends there. We stopped first at the pueblo and climbed the ladders to find Emily alone in their "trailer house." My friend was fascinated with its long narrow rooms connecting their living, eating, and sleeping areas so high up on the third floor. Although Emily was pleased to meet my friend, she couldn't hide her uneasiness. When I said I was sorry Harriet couldn't meet Eliseo, Emily didn't answer but seemed relieved when we decided to go. Later, I found out that on that day there was a special ceremonial not open to the public, and Eliseo had already left for the kiva. I was sure Emily had feared she'd have to ask us to leave.

Later, as we continued the tour to see the historic adobe church at Ranchos de Taos and to visit with the Fosters, Harriet realized she'd left her purse at the pueblo. We drove back to find the entrance blocked by two solemn Indians, their arms crossed on their chests. Although we told them what had happened and insisted we had to get Harriet's purse, they responded that the pueblo was closed. I later wrote to Emily, who explained and sent the purse by mail.

Another time I had the privilege of attending a family christening ceremony at Taos Pueblo. I was a Saturday night guest of a hometown friend who was staying at Ranchos de San Geronimo in Taos. On Sunday morning I decided to visit Emily and Eliseo before returning to Santa Fe and drove out to the pueblo. Eliseo's father, a distinguished old man with deep wrinkles lining his hollow cheeks, recognized me and said, "They're out at their ranch, but you'll never find it. I'll get someone to go with you."

Two little Indian boys were proud to show me the way; and we found Eliseo with his braids tied up around his head, cultivating corn. Eliseo awakened Emily, who was sleeping under a big cottonwood tree. Then, pleasantly surprised by our visit, he brought us a glass of illegal wine from a jug he kept hidden. During lunch Emily said, "Vi, we're going to have to go back to the pueblo this afternoon. My sister's new daughter is being baptized. But you can come with us if you want to." I felt honored to be invited and looked forward to the ceremony.

When we came to her sister's home at the pueblo, I was introduced to the people gathered for the occasion. Although I was impressed by some of the elderly men and women with wrinkles channeling their dark faces, their solemnity made me wonder whether they approved of my presence. As I stood in the back during the traditional christening ceremony, I was captivated by Emily's darling little niece, after which we moved to a crowded room filled by three tables solidly covered by plates of food featuring corn and chile. Through it all, I had many questions but maintained my good behavior.

On another occasion, Emily and Eliseo's only daughter Josephine was married, and I was pleased to be invited to the wedding. Once again, during the ceremony I had many questions to which I could not get answers. I wondered how the men could have their own secret religious ceremonies in the kiva but let a white priest officiate at a family wedding ceremony in the Catholic church near the edge of the pueblo. I did learn that before the ceremony the bride traditionally spent a special designated time with her grandmother, who no doubt passed down cultural traditions and family wisdom.

Another unexpected connection with the Tewas of Taos Pueblo came through Mary's family friendship with Mabel Dodge Luhan. When we were in Taos, Mary pointed out the several homes that Mabel of the Dodge fortune had built in earlier years before settling at Los Gallos, the house named for Mabel's decorative Mexican ceramic roosters. Writer Natalie Goldberg once said that Los Gallos condensed and crystallized the presence of Taos.

Today, the twenty-two-room Los Gallos is a National Historical Landmark. Over the Internet people can read fascinating stories about its intriguing early history and unbelievable design, or call an 800 number to rent one of ten guest rooms, or register for a workshop on meditation or creativity renewal, or even just have an expensive dinner there. I never did visit Los Gallos, and especially regret not seeing the colorful bathroom with windows painted in quasi-petroglyph style by D. H. Lawrence.

Instead, when I was in the Southwest Mary and I visited Mabel at a home she had built in later years at the confluence of the Embudo River and the Rio Grande south of Taos. At that time her health was failing, and we dropped by with food for her special diet. It was difficult from knowing her then to visualize her earlier life as a pioneering socialite; but learning about that earlier life actually changed mine.

I discovered that Mabel had grown up in a wealthy New England family, attending a private school that groomed women for marriage and family, with little allowance for fulfillment of individual dreams. In rebellion, Mabel became a national and international symbol of the sexually emancipated, self-determined woman in control of her own destiny.

After the accidental death of her first husband in 1905, Mabel gained financial freedom in marrying Edwin Dodge, who took her to live in Florence. There she spent her time reaching out to the European art world. By 1912, she was dissatisfied with what she felt was a life of form without content, and they returned to New York City. In the pre-World War I days, her address of 25 Fifth Avenue became internationally known as a stimulating gathering place for prominent intellectuals, writers, and activists with avant-garde ideas, including A. A. Brill, Walter Lippmann, Max Eastman, Lincoln Steffens, and Margaret Sanger. It was a group of people who rejoiced in their sexuality, and had hopes of bringing about harmony in a nonexploitive economic world.

When the war scattered much of her coterie and brought on a conservative backlash, this emancipated woman abruptly abandoned her career as New York socialite and arts patron. It was then that her third husband, Maurice Sterne, felt she might better fulfill her dreams in New Mexico. As a result, they moved to Taos, where Mabel did indeed find in the culture of the Pueblo Indians a supreme example of her ideal—in the model of their beautiful, six-hundred-year-old community with its profound social, artistic, and religious values.

In Santa Fe there was controversy about Mabel's role in a notorious art community at Taos. Some saw her coterie as an extraordinary group of questionable rich intellectuals. It included famous writers and artists like D. H. Lawrence, Carl Jung, Max Weber, Willa Cather, Leopold Stokowski, Martha

Graham, Paul and Rebecca Strand (who brought Georgia O'Keeffe with them), John Marin, Marsden Hartley, and Andrew Dasburg. Stories often revolved about her having used money, womanly wiles, and willful independence to attract and influence the elite art world. She had a reputation as a wealthy tyrannical hostess who had a way of attracting artists and writers through what Ansel Adams called her "talons for talent," offering them a refuge from the materialistic mainstream and a place to nurture their creativity.

In 1923, shortly after her arrival in Taos, Mabel cut her hair, started wearing serapes, and fell in love with and later married Antonio Luhan, a full-blooded Taos Indian. Tony seemed to give her the kind of personal acceptance she had not found in her own family or in the intellectual art world.

Later, because of Mabel's heartfelt beliefs in their way of life, she thought the Pueblo Indians could be a bridge between American culture based on a national obsession with power and material possession and a new American culture to come. With their lack of interest in material wealth or personal achievement, their devotion to communal values that bound them together in pueblos, and a healthy religious respect for the natural environment, Mabel felt this bridge could help Taos become the birthplace for a new American culture—that the Pueblo Indian values had an important message for the frenetic white race heading for self-destruction. This feeling was later reinforced as she watched the harnessing of atomic energy into bombs at the nearby Los Alamos National Laboratory.

Mabel promoted her beliefs by using the talented artists, writers, and reformers she had enticed to Taos: John Marin, Georgia O'Keeffe, and Andrew Dasburg to record the beauty of the Taos landscape for the ages; Leopold Stokowski to capture the essence of Native Indian music; John Collier, U.S. commissioner of Indian affairs to protect Indian lands and culture; and Robinson Jeffers and D. H. Lawrence to spread her social and political beliefs in poetry and fiction.

Mabel did realize the paradox of her championing simple

Pueblo Indian principles and values while at the same time living a life of affluence, which brought resentment by young Indians returning from World War II who organized to get better heat and plumbing at the pueblo. In her 1924 memoirs, Mabel said she felt redeemed through the love of Tony Luhan, and that through her own life's efforts hoped to bring about the destruction of the system of which she'd been a part. In sharing his Indian life Tony was a spiritual mentor to some of Mabel's guests, like Willa Cather. Many felt Cather based her Eusablo on Tony in her *Death Comes for the Archbishop*. In addition, Georgia O'Keeffe took off on many trips with Tony because she shared his love of the country.

When I knew Mabel, she was very protective of Tony. On one visit, I discovered she had him in the hospital for an operation on an ingrown toenail—an excuse for keeping him away from a pueblo ceremonial retreat. Once every ten years the men at Taos Pueblo had a kiva retreat for forty days and nights, sleeping on the cold ground. Mabel felt this would not be good for Tony at his age. Later, I learned that this was one of the secret ceremonies that involved continence and fasting.

In living with so many questions about the intriguing Pueblo culture, I was fascinated to read in Tony Hillerman's *The Spell of New Mexico* that Swiss psychiatrist Carl Jung also found Pueblo Indians unusually secretive about religious matters and thus abandoned any attempt at direct questioning. In trying to discover some fundamental principles of their religion, he would make remarks, watch their responses, and note that when he hit on something essential, emotion was evident, sometimes even tears.

It seemed to Jung that Pueblo religious beliefs were not theories but eternal realities—not something you preached but something you lived. He did learn that instead of a Father God they have a Father Sun, who keeps the stars and the moon moving in perfect order, and that as individuals they also play a part in this daily ritual, not only for themselves but for the whole world. Jung felt that such beliefs brought the Pueblo

Indians together in a religious community that would continue as long as their mysteries were kept.*

Another writer, George Wharton James, added to my
knowledge about Pueblo Indians in his *New Mexico: The Land
of the Delight Makers*—a masterful book of the 1920s covering
endless aspects I'd wondered about. Although I realize that
much may have changed in more than half a century, I found
that at least then there was a basic tenent of Pueblo religion
that speaks to all of us today: "Thou shall acknowledge the
wonder!" The Tewas feel that our human and natural world is
the result of sexual union, to them a matter of religious devotion that encompasses their Father Sun and their Mother
Earth. According to James, the Pueblo Indians of his day saw
no evil and had a superior sexual morality with no self-con-
sciousness.

The more I read about the culture of the Pueblo Indians,
the more their culture suggested answers to numerous over-
whelming problems we face in our civilized society—a view
that paralleled what Mabel Dodge Luhan and D. H. Lawrence
had also discovered in their relationship with Tony Luhan and
his people.

I'd see this in their acknowledgment of the wonder; in religious worship of the natural sexual world to which we all owe
our very existence; in their lack of aspiration for money, fame,
or power; in the example they set for their children in their
concept of community rather than glorification of the individual; in their view of riches in the natural world belonging to all
of us rather than to individuals; in their meaningful arts and
crafts; in practices of natural and mystical healing; and in their
moral maturity, reflected in rituals acknowledging the stages
of life.

James saw the Indian world as entirely different from our
rational, scientific, computerized world. In their world, there

---

* Tony Hillerman, *The Spell of New Mexico* (Albuquerque: University of
New Mexico Press, 1984).

Making adobes at Jim
Riley's house.

How to build an
adobe (note *vigas)*.

FORMAL OPENING

SANTA FE NEW MEXICAN
Friday, Feb. 3, 1950

Santa Fe Ski Basin

SANTA FE BASIN OPEN HOUSE
TWO BIG DAYS!

Saturday and Sunday, Feb. 4 and 5

Plan now to attend. There'll be fun for everyone! Caravans will be made up in Federal Place both days and will leave for the Santa Fe Basin promptly at 1 p.m. There will be racing, exhibition skiing, ice skating, free coffee, doughnuts and soft drinks and free rides on the lift as time will allow.

OFFICIAL PROGRAM AND SOUVENIR EDITION

Robert Woods

Opposite: Front page of a special supplement to the *New Mexican* announcing the opening festivities of the Santa Fe Ski Basin.

Above: In front of the ski lodge .

Below: Waiting for the chairlift at the Santa Fe Ski Basin.

On the trail in the Pecos Wilderness.

Mountaintop Penitente crosses seen the last day of the trail ride.

Emily and Eliseo Conchas, the author's friends at Taos Pueblo.

The author's living room window overlooking Canyon Road.

Entrance to the author's 205 Canyon Road apartment.

The author talking with a cowboy in Jimmy Stewart's fiftieth movie, *Man from Laramie*.

Jeff Chandler and Linda Darnell in *Two Flags West* with Joseph Cotton.

Joseph Cotton on the set of *Two Flags West*.

The author's friend Tim Sanders participating in a Pueblo ceremonial dance at Santa Clara Pueblo.

Ristras of bright red chiles drying in the autumn sun, a common harvest time scene in the Indian pueblos and Spanish villages of northern New Mexico.

Airline stewardesses at the Santa Fe Airport for the Resort Roundup during the days when major airlines served the city.

Airline employees participating in the Resort Roundup at La Posada Inn. (The author is in the front row, center)..

Burro Alley, where Polly and Thornton Carswell built the first Shed Restaurant.

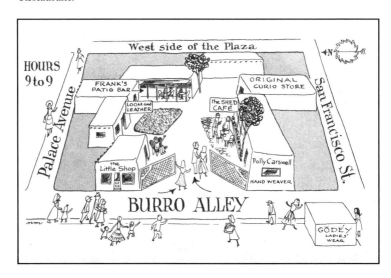

LEFT: Polly Carswell cooking at Hyde Park Lodge, where Violet forst met her.

BELOW: The Carswells at home on Rodriguiz Street in Santa Fe with their son Courtney, who later operated The Shed at Prince Plaza with his father Thornton.

The author's apartment behind 202 Canyon Road, the first house on the left after crossing the Santa Fe River.

was power in mountains, rivers, rocks, and all living things. It was a mythic world, arising out of the natural world with integral powers in the human realm.

James greatly added to my understanding when he mentioned that Catholic or Protestant rituals, although difficult for some to understand or accept, could be learned. In contrast, he felt half a lifetime would be required to begin to grasp the significance of Pueblo Indian symbolism basic to the religion in their daily lives. Their world was bounded geographically and mythically by four sacred mountains, where holy men would go on pilgrimages to pray for rain, to gather medicinal herbs, or to carry out cultural rituals at puberty or other stages of life.[*]

I also learned from Native American writers Tom and Richard Hill in their book *Creation's Journey: Native American Identity and Beliefs*. They felt many Indians are skeptical about the white man's Bering Strait theory, and believe the legends that say they were created from the earth itself, the water, or from the stars. According to them, the land was the first of five gifts received from their ancestors and must be shared with future generations. The second gift was the power and spirit that animals shared with people by providing them with food, clothing, and shelter. The third and fourth gifts were the spirit forces we little understand—concerning family and community relationships throughout life and survival after death. The fifth gift was a sense of identity—expressed and sustained through dress, art, family, and tribal traditions.[†]

Ironically, it was the very people who had come to America for religious freedom who denied that freedom to the Native Americans, who have suffered over the years as we've tried to make them like us. Yet in their history Native Americans leave for us today a living example of a life-sustaining culture we are

---

[*] George Warton James, *New Mexico: The Land of the Delight Makers* (Page Co., 1920).
[†] Tom and Richard Hill, *Creation's Journey: Native American Identity and Beliefs* (Washington, D.C.: Smithsonian Institution Press, 1994).

learning the hard way to reclaim.

In thinking of my Taos Pueblo friends, over and over again I began to perceive that many of our present-day problems arise out of our European and Middle Eastern backgrounds. We view ourselves as the center of the universe, with the Christian Bible giving us power over all of nature, while the Pueblo Indians see themselves as part of that nature in harmony with the birds and animals, mountains, the sun and moon. They lack our personal ego that stresses ambition, attainment, and material wealth; instead, they see value in peace, generosity, brotherhood, community participation, and responsibility.

Today, I am pleased to see how Indians have taken the initiative in managing their culture and destiny. Beginning with their move to take advantage of treaty rights in the recent operation of casinos, they are speaking out in a quiet but impressive way. Cherokee Chief Wilma Mankiller, the first woman to be elected to that office, said on a radio program in 1987 that no one will solve their problems for them, but that they will plot their course and do it themselves.

I thought of what she said as I learned that in 1990 it was found that the Bill of Rights for the free expression of religion was not extended to the Native American Church because of its sacramental use of the drug peyote. Then prime mover Reuben Snake went to work and brought about the revision of this prohibition with the passage by Congress of the American Indian Religious Freedom Act Amendments of 1994, which President Clinton signed into Public Law 103-344 on October 6, 1994.

Meeting and reading about Mable Dodge Lujan was not only important for my understanding of Pueblo Indian culture but for my perspective on the modern world. I had Mary to thank for having known Mabel, another gift from my rich Canyon Road days. If it hadn't been for this opportunity, I might have only seen Mabel as a spoiled little rich girl pushing her individual freedoms, instead of later identifying with her. As a single woman I had been able to make decisions that removed me from the traditional roles of women of my time as Mabel had; I also agreed with Mabel's long-range visions for one world in many fundamental ways. Hers were human values which have a prophetic note. I felt this even more deeply when recently Skinner House Books in Boston published *A Modern Pioneer*, about my years as a Unitarian minister. On the dust jacket it says, "Each of Kochendoerfer's ministries tackled controversial social and political issues that soon defined a dynamic era in American history—gay and lesbian rights, the Vietnam War, civil rights, reproductive rights, and the disintegration of the family."

Interestingly, back in the 1950s I heard an anecdote showing another side of Mabel Dodge Luhan. One day after I had returned from work the phone rang. It was Jim Riley at the Chamber of Commerce, who said, "Vi, two *Life* photographers came in after you left. They would like a couple of gals to take to dinner. Would you and Mary like to go?" Of course we would! So Jim brought John Bryson and Peter Stackpole over to our apartment, and they joined us for a drink.

We learned they had come to get photos of our six-foot-seven corporation commissioner, who had been sleeping on the capitol steps the previous two weeks so he could file first and get his name on the top of the ballot for governor. In those days ballots were printed in English and Spanish; and since there were so many Martinezes and Chavezes, being on top was politically strategic.

When Jim left, Peter said, "Come on, John. Let's get our pictures, and then we'll come back and pick the gals up." But we wanted to go along; so they let us hold flashbulbs as they took lots of pictures from different angles. Then we raced the film out to the airport before going to dinner.

It was a delightful evening with great conversation. John told of his prize photo of an old man who had died on the plains of Texas and who was found days later, his faithful dog at his side. They told of pranks photographers played on each

----

other, saying, "One time we got a shot of a guy's bare back side, blew it up to four by four and sent it to him in a big wooden crate."

Then John told how Mabel Dodge Luhan had cheated him out of a big scoop some years back because he went to the wrong two women first: "I was writing on the three loves of D. H. Lawrence, but I went to Dorothy Brett and his wife Frieda to get their story. All three loved D. H. and competed for his attention and affection. I heard sometime ago that Mabel was so eager to keep Lawrence nearby she deeded a small ranch to Frieda, thinking that might make them stay. Then friends were shocked when Frieda Lawrence gave Mabel the original manuscript of *Sons and Lovers*. I even heard that when Lawrence died, Mabel got part of his ashes, placed them in a cement block, and put it in a shrine built for him at the ranch. Now I realize I should have checked things out and gone to Mabel first."

The New Mexico political climate of the 1950s that had brought John and Peter to Santa Fe involved payoffs and questionable regulations at polls. The uniqueness of this political corruption lay in the fact that its activities were largely out in the open. For example, one time I was invited to a luncheon at the home of the woman who headed the Republican Party in Santa Fe. After lunch, a small group sat at a table with a stack of ten dollar bills, deciding how many to put in each special envelope for certain precincts—to buy votes. Big limos were also provided to give rides to poor Spanish people without cars.

Since all these activities were accepted as politics New Mexico style, we actually looked forward to elections. Each time, as we listened to returns, we would make bets on the time of the inevitable announcement from one particular area in which there seemed to be perpetual political controversy, "The ballot boxes of Rio Arriba County have been impounded!" And I remember the story I heard of a wealthy eastern senator, who after losing reelection in his home state, moved to New Mexico. There, with the relatively small number of voters and the ability openly to buy votes, he bought himself a New Mexico seat in the United States Senate.

When I was in Santa Fe, the League of Women Voters initiated the idea of candidate meetings. In the beginning, the meetings were boycotted by some of the old Spanish candidates because such meetings had never been held before. Later, they began to realize it was to their advantage to appear and began to ask, "Who are these ladies?"

Just after the elections in 1954, my new experiences living with Mary came to an end. After I had inherited the wonderful relationship when her earlier roommate had married, Mary's Ohio boyfriend persuaded her to marry him. With a lovely picture of Mary, the article in the *New Mexican* said about the wedding, "Justice and Mrs. Henry A. Kiker announce the marriage of Mrs. Kiker's daughter, Mary Pollard, to Dinsmore Wheeler of Cleveland, Ohio, in Chicago May 1." This brought a big change in my life.

Those years on Canyon Road with Mary were filled with unique learning experiences which blended the aspects of three cultures into an extraordinary mosaic of patterns I shall never forget. From Mary's political family I had learned about New Mexico society and politics. I smiled as I thought of the new hat and gloves I had had to buy when her mother insisted we attend legislative teas. Because of Mary I had been immersed in the rich tricultural traditions, getting to know individual Indian, Spanish, and creative people up and down the Rio Grande Valley from Taos to Albuquerque.

Mary was a much-loved person who was at home in the governor's mansion or the simplest adobe shack. She had a talent for creating harmony wherever she went. I recall attending a meeting with her in Taos. As we walked into a small adobe building, we could hear loud controversy down the hall. But when she entered the room and joined the group, Mary's opening gambit dissipated the tension and made everyone smile. When she left Santa Fe, she was missed by many people, but I smiled as I read Mary's first letter from Ohio, in which she said, "Vi, up here everything is green!"

After Mary's departure, I did not want to stay in the large apartment by myself, and the owners, Carl and Wilma Jensen, let me move into one of the two guest houses behind the big house after I returned from a summer vacation in Minnesota.

Once you entered my new apartment through the kitchen, there was a large living room on the left and a bath and bedroom on the right. I could use the driveway on the left, just across the Santa Fe River bridge. The road continued along the riverside of the big house at 202 Canyon Road and swung down around the front of my new apartment to an open carport under big trees along the Santa Fe River, which I could see from my kitchen window. Out of my living room windows, I could view the large sloping garden Carl Jensen's lovable old father kept in bloom with lovely flowers throughout the year. Beyond the garden was Canyon Road, where I could still see all the activity in the most visited area of Santa Fe. At that time the area across Canyon Road along the Alameda was covered with a forest of small trees.

When I visited there some years ago, that beautiful homey corner at 202 Canyon Road was gone, as was our apartment, which is part of the sprawling main house. I heard it had once been an insurance agency office, but was then a boutique, with our old living room filled with women's clothes.

Lines of cars buzzed past on the nearby four-lane Paseo de Peralta, carrying traffic in a wide circle around the city. Gone was Castillo Street, on which I had walked to work. When I was there, Castillo had led into Canyon Road from Palace Avenue, with St. Francis Parochial School on the corner with Alameda. Then as Canyon Road bent to the left across the Santa Fe River, a tiny end of Castillo kept straight on to dead end at De Vargas, which went further to the left into Canyon Road. This all made a tiny triangle on the map back then, and it was difficult to believe the pictures I later received which showed a row of adobe shops along Canyon Road on the left all the way from the river, filling up the entire area where our garden had been.

During the time I lived in Santa Fe, there were many tales about activities on Canyon Road. There were stories about the Canyon Road bridge being a secret spot under which the Rosenbergs had passed early atomic secrets. Although reports by Russian spies corroborated the stories at the fiftieth anniversary of the bomb, recently this information has been questioned by the KGB.

Canyon Road was also the home of many artists of the early Santa Fe art colony. This colony had been preceded by a group of scholars and anthropologists like Adolph Bandelier, a Swiss scholar of international renown, who had lived in Santa Fe in the 1880s and inspired a revival of the Spanish Pueblo architectural style. By the 1920s, the Santa Fe art colony outnumbered the scholars and became a major force in Santa Fe life, bringing more Anglo influence to the city.

Almost as historically famous for its artists as Canyon Road was Camino del Monte Sol, which branched off to the right a way up. This was the street where Los Cinco Pintores (The Five Painters) lived—a spirited group influenced by Cezanne and post-impressionists. Along with several other painters and artists, Los Cinco Pintores had built homes on this street. When they had first moved to the undeveloped street, it was called Telephone Road; but the artists resented this unpoetic name and renamed the street after a nearby mountain.

Members of Los Cinco Pintores who settled Camino del Monte Sol were Jozel Bakos, Fremont Ellis, Walter Mruk, Willard Nash, and Will Schuster, the creator of Zozobra. In the 1920s, they had reacted against the international avant-garde group Mabel Dodge Luhan had attracted to Taos, labeling them "radical."

Throughout the Depression and during the 1950s, the Santa Fe art colony grew slowly. Then in the 1960s Santa Fe began to be more of a tourist enclave, with restaurants and small shops opening in pockets along Canyon Road to attract tourists with books, paintings, and southwestern art objects. On a recent trip there, I visited the studio of Gian Andrea, showing liturgical arts at 626 Canyon Road, where Drew Bacigalupa gave me a copy of his book *Journal of an Itinerant Artist.*

That day, after leaving crowded Canyon Road, my friend and I explored the big warehouse-like buildings that were overflowing with southwestern wares to attract visitors. I remembered the time in the 1950s when the old Five Points Liquor Store was located in the middle of the intersection of Five Corners. In those days we would dam up the Santa Fe River across from the telephone building and hang huge canvases between the trees during the day to keep the sun from melting the ice. Then we would come down in the evening and skate or stand around a small fire sipping hot drinks. As I reminisced, I once again was grateful to Mary for sharing with me so much of the old magic.

CHAPTER 5

- -

PROMOTING SANTA FE
TOURISM and FILMMAKING

In the fall of 1952, I was sitting at my desk at the Chamber of Commerce when a handsome young man in a maroon sweater walked in asking for information on dude ranches. Although the Northern New Mexico Resort Association was a member of the Chamber of Commerce, I said, "It's too late in the season. They're not hiring anyone now." The young man smiled and said, "But I'm not looking for a job. I want to stay at one." That was a different story.

I thought of the ranches nearby, most of which catered to wealthy Texan families and would not be attractive to a young man. Finally, I decided on Rancho del Monte, and called Jim Field, who said he would be in about four that afternoon to pick him up. So the young man left, had lunch, and then returned to wait.

We had a long talk, and I learned he was Jim Madison from Chicago. "I drove out to California with my buddy in his old Ford jalopy, and now I'm on my way home," he said. "I have a couple of weeks before I leave for Switzerland to study city planning at a college there." Then he told me his father owned a large car dealership in Chicago and had planned for him to take over; but Jim did not find that option appealing.

Later that week, aspen season was at its height. I called a couple of friends to drive up the mountain to see the annual golden glory, only to be put off by things like, "I just have to wash my hair." Then I thought of Jim, and called Rancho del Monte to find he was sitting near the phone. When I asked whether he would like to drive up to the Ski Basin, he said, "You bet. I was just trying to find something to do."

I picked him up, and our spirits were lifted high all the way up the mountain road. After exclaiming over and over again at the breathtaking patterns of quaking golden aspens against the azure New Mexico sky, we walked around the basin area, took pictures, and then just sat there breathing in nature's gifts.

After supper at my apartment, Jim and I visited Helen and Foster Hyatt, a couple I had met through Audrey and Al, who lived in a historic adobe more than 250 years old. From the road you couldn't see the house at all since it was beyond a high adobe wall with a wide double wooden gate. Inside the wall was a long yard in front of an extended weathered adobe. The house was in two parts, connected by a small open-arched patio with a colorful tiled niche, a fountain in the center, and a wrought-iron gate opening into a backyard leading down to the Santa Fe River. I learned later that this connecting patio was one of the most photographed spots of the city, with many promoters using it to say, "This is old Santa Fe!"

Foster told us about the Spanish family they had bought it from, mentioning that the longest part to the left, which seemed to go on and on through living room, kitchen, bedrooms, and into what they now used as a garage, was an example of how the Spanish kept building on room after room as a family grew. The wing to the right of the patio was Foster's studio. He explained to Jim that it had the original mud and blood floor, which to us looked like a shiny deep brown waxed linoleum.

Foster was a delineator and worked with several of the local architects. He told us about coming to Santa Fe years before, when he learned that former schoolmates Kenneth Clark and Willard Kruger were working there, and explained what it was like in those days.

"When we first arrived in Santa Fe, we found a small city of around eight thousand people—mostly Spanish. About every third one spoke only Spanish. Our first home was across from the Masonic Temple on Washington Avenue. It had been the home of Silvanus Morley, the archaeologist who started the discoveries of ancient sites in Central America. The house was also said to be the former residence of the armor of the Spanish garrison, and contained the ruins of an old Indian pueblo. The library there was a revelation to us!

"Then after returning to Texas, we came back to Santa Fe in 1943. Helen started a search for a home. One October day coming out Upper Canyon Road, with cottonwoods yellow and chamisa in full bloom, she came into the large patio here at 1579 and immediately knew that this would be it.

"Vi, you're one of the bunch that have started coming in after World War II, and you all are bound to make a difference. I heard a month or so ago that actress Shirley MacLaine had plans to build a mansion up on top of Atalaya Mountain; but it seems some organized local effort stopped that. Anyway, we still feel that we are a part of the real old Santa Fe here on Upper Canyon Road. We hope it can stay this way a long time."

After a delightful evening with the Hyatts, Jim spent the night on my living room sofa, and I drove him back to Rancho del Monte the following day. Later, he wrote me from Switzerland, and from Chicago after he returned there to open a record shop with a friend.

In the 1950s, more and more tourists and residents came to Santa Fe attracted by the landscape and culture we promoted at the Chamber of Commerce. The Northern New Mexico Resort Association was one of our members; but at first most of the guests at our surrounding ranches were from Texas, and old Santa Feans often remarked, "We don't like the Texans, but we like their money." Employed at the Chamber of Commerce, I dreamed up the idea of reaching beyond Texas to promote the City Different by inviting representatives of airlines as well as train and bus lines serving Santa Fe to come see what we had to offer vacationists. This spawned what came to be known as the Resort Roundup.

In the 1950s, Santa Fe was serviced regularly by TWA, and people at the Chamber of Commerce enjoyed very friendly relationships with TWA personnel. Buck Riordan, our Albuquerque TWA representative, and practically family at the

Chamber of Commerce, really turned out TWAers for the Roundup: the general manager, the sales manager, and chief reservations woman from New York City; their West Coast advertising executive from Los Angeles; their TV and radio men; and reservation women from Chicago, Kansas City, and San Francisco. There were also a few VIPs, public relation and advertising men, and hostesses from Pioneer and Continental Airlines, as well as a few men from the Santa Fe Railroad. All in all, there were twenty-six men and eighteen women.

Most attending the Roundup flew in on a Thursday. Meeting, welcoming, and billeting made for a busy day. The kickoff was a cocktail party and buffet dinner at La Fonda Hotel. Some guests began to learn the hard way the alcohol-altitude lesson even before we left La Fonda that evening to go to El Nido Night Club north of town. As guests were feeling good, the group singing began. TWA Buck had a terrific voice and loved my harmonizing.

Since one of the women at the Chamber of Commerce was on vacation, I had to work Friday, and joined the group on Saturday in Taos. There I heard raves about the red-carpet treatment the group had enjoyed at several of the ranches. Most of the representatives I talked with were fascinated with the adobe buildings—particularly mentioning La Fonda Hotel. Others loved the rolling countryside dotted with pincushions of piñon. Fortunately, the weather was perfect to show off our clear blue sky and red rocks in a way New Yorkers probably had never seen the area before. I especially called the weather to their attention, hoping they would remember to tell other New Yorkers when they returned.

While at Taos, women were billeted at Taos Inn, a weathered adobe near the Plaza, where we all gathered in the patio, cocktails in hand, to watch three Taos Indians doing the Squaw Dance around a big fire. We then joined in the dance, holding hands and stomping around the fire in a big circle. Hunger was satisfied with a fabulous dinner at El Rancho San Geronimo, after which we went out to sprawling Sagebrush Inn for the rest of the evening of drinking and dancing.

Since Sagebrush Inn was a great example of northern New Mexico architecture, its interesting design impressed our visitors from more traditional areas. In addition to attractive sleeping accommodations off long portals, it had a large lobby, a dining area featuring gourmet food, and an unusual cocktail lounge. It also offered its guests trail rides and pack trips into nearby mountains with fine hunting and fishing.

We spent most of the evening in a small lounge attached to a huge bar. The TWA general manager was at a little round table with a Taos man. In a high mood, he was telling the man from Taos how much he liked the country, and then asked, "But just what do you do for a living up here?" "I raise chinchillas," said the man. The manager's face lit up as the Taos man continued, "My ranch is just a few miles from here. Would you like to come out to see my chinchillas?" The TWA general manager said he would, and they left. Less than fifteen minutes later we were surprised to see the manager return alone, sobered by the learning experience of taking off with a gay man. I always wondered what kind of story he told back in New York City, as well as the story the TWA general sales manager told, who was also flying high and made some kind of arrangement to take over the bar. His pouring of drinks without measure must have given the Sagebrush Inn a big write-off.

Although women had many invitations to spend the night at Sagebrush Inn, most of us went back to our rooms at Taos Inn, where we had piles of piñon beside our kiva fireplaces. We needed a fire that night, and experienced that never-to-be-forgotten piñon fragrance of the Southwest.

The Resort Roundup was a big success and no doubt contributed to the increasing popularity of Santa Fe—the impetus for the changing of the old Santa Fe I now so decry. We at the Chamber of Commerce promoted package deals not only for skiers who, like me, had never dreamed of skiing in New Mexico. The news of our high mountain trails and dry powder snow lasting into late spring brought skiers by train from as far east as Kansas City, and even further by air. The Chamber of Commerce later had similar promotional events for airline groups when Ghost Ranch was opened to the public.

That fall I had an unusual experience in more remote parts of New Mexico. One day Jim Riley put a brochure on my desk, saying, "Read this, Vi. Each year the American Forestry Association sponsors this trail ride in the Pecos Wilderness. People come from the East Coast and the West Coast, but no one from here has ever gone. You might think about it." I did, and as I looked over the material, this is what I read: "Expedition No. 17—Pecos Wilderness, Santa Fe National Forest, New Mexico. September 9 to 20, 1953. Headquarters: Hotel La Posada, Santa Fe, New Mexico. Cost: $215 from Santa Fe." I became more interested, and read on:

> The first day calls for a 46-mile drive to Cowles and six miles horseback to the first camp at Horse Thief Meadows. The next includes a big 16-mile loop from camp to Lake Katherine in a beautiful, inspiring setting on the slopes of Santa Fe Baldy, via Stewart Lake, alternating through heavy timber and open meadow. Then a 16-mile day over a pass to Panchewela Creek and over a low divide to the Rio Medio, with a long climb to the divide of the Sangre de Cristos for wonderful views. Camp that day is near the shore of Pecos Baldy Lake at nearly 12,000 feet, known for good fishing.
>
> Day Four is either a rest day, or one may opt for a ride to the foot of Truches Peak and then a two-mile hike up to the top of this second highest peak in New Mexico with a tremendous view from 13,300 feet. Next, a 17-mile ride north under the divide through alpine meadows and open spruce timber past Trail Riders Wall and under Truches Peak, down Rio Azul to Beatty's Cabin, with facilities for hot basin baths and general clean up.
>
> A 14-mile trip out from there next day is over the top of the Cerrito Padre, then crossing the head of the Rito Maestas through open parks intermingled with heavy

timber and on to the Santa Barbara Divide for lunch. Then down the Pecos River past the falls and return to Beatty's Cabin.

The seventh day is a day of rest, or a ride following along the canyon wall of the picturesque Pecos Box, arriving in a valley of small lakes formed by dams constructed by a large beaver colony over a period of years. The party will then proceed up the canyon and climb out on the east side, returning along Hamilton Mesa to a high point overlooking many miles of the historic Pecos River, with scenes, photographs of which have graced the cover of many outdoor magazines.

A short 8-mile ride is scheduled for the next day, before Day Nine, a strenuous day for riders and horses up a steep trail to Elk Mountain Divide, with a gradual descent down to the old historical Harvey Ranch and further to camp on Hollinger Creek deep in a canyon. Then, after a day of rest 15 more miles down the Hollinger and up Beaver Creek past rocky points to the knife-edge ridge to Hermit's Peak, with a breath-taking view to the east from this historic peak where Penitentes have carried and erected heavy log crosses at Easter time for nearly a century. Then, the last day, after seeing the sunrise and the hidden cave of the hermit, the party will descend a sensational trail with nearly a hundred switchbacks to the valley and Gallines Ranger Station. From there the group will drive the 78 miles back to Santa Fe.

I reveled at the wilderness descriptions and the lovely Spanish names of rivers and peaks. Since I was always looking for new experiences, I signed up and started accumulating all kinds of clothes and gear I would need. I checked with Tom Olds and Doug O'Bannon, friends who were owners of Brush Ranch and Mountain View Ranch, who were outfitting the trip. They assured me I didn't have to be an expert rider; since most of the trip was walking on mountain trails, and that a pack train would go ahead to set up individual shepherd's tents and get ready to feed us dinners and breakfasts, with lunches usually picnic style on the trail.

The first night out in the high country was at Horse Thief Meadows after a short six-mile ride. Happy Ley and the crew had gotten there early and landed eastern brook trout, which we had for a great dinner, along with steaks. Waking up next morning brought disbelief as I found frost on the outside of my tent. As I shivered down to the creek, brushing my teeth in ice water, I thought to myself, "And I paid good money for this!"

Breakfast changed all that. It was surely a time to remember. If you've never tasted a dried Japanese mushroom omelet in the Sangre de Cristo Mountains, watching the sun peek over the mountaintops, you've never lived! Tom's omelets were manna from heaven. Other mornings we had flapjacks, bacon and eggs, and fried potatoes.

We rode from eight to twenty miles a day in this wilderness wonderland, where no roads are allowed and Beatty's Cabin was the only shelter of any kind. There were two rest days; but I never rested. There were mountain lakes or trout streams where I learned to outwit the wily trout under the tutelage of no less than Elliot Barker, a retired state game warden. He, Bob Ground, and J. W. Johnson (who were both non-college-degree rangers) knew and loved every inch of that fabulous high country. And they shared that love with us in so many memorable ways.

Temperatures varied tremendously. When the sun was out, we would sometimes peel down to a cotton shirt. When it disappeared, we would reach for a jacket. By the time it was dark at nearly ll,000 feet, it was near freezing, so we had campfires to end all campfires. The wranglers would cut long thick logs and drag them into a square for us to sit on around a huge fire. There was always a big log we kept pushing into the fire as it burned. This suggests the size of our fires, which were nevertheless dwarfed by the tall fir trees. I was happy that my friend Dave had insisted against my protests that I take his fiberglass-lined jacket. It had zippers on the sides and across the waistline, so I could let down a welcome back pad to sit on. We sang our hearts out to Ethel's guitar, our voices rising in the clear, cold night air along with fire sparks between towering fir trees. With regular requests for firewater, we kept warm by passing the bottle around the square.

We came to know what the weather man meant when he said, "Scattered showers in the mountains," as we became accustomed to transferring bright yellow slickers from the neat rolls behind the saddle to our shoulders. We were wary at each thunderclap, since we sometimes had to cope with horses rearing up on their hind legs.

The weather often made our ride more adventurous. In the high country, thunderstorms can be a harrowing experience, like on our day off when we were camped at Pecos Baldy Lake and some of us climbed Truches Peak. There was no warning of a storm that day since it was sunny when we began the two-mile climb, after riding as far as we could and then tying the horses. We could only move slowly over huge boulders, and after half an hour or more, clouds began to form. Although it did not rain, we were squeamish as we felt a kind of tickling in the hair on top of our heads. Just then, Mark, one of the men who'd been ahead, came sliding toward us, low down on his backside, wild-eyed and yelling, "Get down, you crazy girls! It got Doc, and it'll get you!"

We asked, "What do you mean, it got Doc? Is he dead?" With teeth chattering, Mark replied, "Well, I just wasn't waiting around to find out." We squatted down as he continued, "Lightning struck close to where Doc was standing. It knocked him down."

Then Mark left us to ride back into camp for help. It turned out that Doc needed this help to return to camp. When the lightning had struck so close to him, he had involuntarily tensed his muscles so tightly that he could not relax. For the rest of the trip, he could not bend to tie his shoelaces, and had trouble getting into his sleeping bag. We also learned that the tickling we'd felt was actually static electrical current playing around in our hair, since we were at 13,100 feet atop the second highest point in New Mexico!

The trip emphasized our common humanity aside from professions. Our group consisted of eighteen doctors, lawyers, executives, housewives, secretaries, and farmers, ranging in age from twenty-two to seventy-two. After the first day out, I would have defied any stranger to pick out the doctor, the executive, or the housewife. And we soon pigeonholed the gripers and complainers, and kept our distance.

With no daily bath or shave, pressed shirts or clean sheets, newspapers, radio or television, we began to enjoy the freedom of complete disregard of personal appearance, national problems, world strife, or the high cost of living. I can still picture riding a sunny stretch high up on the way to Pecos Baldy, exalting in the expansive vistas, the quiet and peacefulness, and thinking, "Out there in the world we live in, little men are fighting each other."

The trip turned out to be one of the highlights of my time in New Mexico. *New Mexico Sun Trails,* a magazine I always thought of back then as a poor man's *Arizona's Highways,* had asked me to write a story about the trip and used some of my color slides. I described the ending of that unforgettable trip in the last two paragraphs of my article "Trail Riders of America Ride the Pecos Wilderness":

> And after the last night at Hermit's Peak, where we sat around the campfire and listened to the sobering legend of the religious recluse known as the Hermit, and the story of the Penitentes, who carried their crude wooden crosses on pilgrimages to the top of this sheer-cliffed 10,100-foot mesa, to leave them as gaunt reminders—and after Sunday morning, when we rolled out of sleeping bags at 5:30 to watch the sun rise across the Las Vegas plains, a rosy glow against the dark silhouettes of the three rugged Penitente crosses at the edge of the cliff—I rode down the nearly hundred switchbacks off Hermit's Peak with a feeling of reverence, dignity, and freshness of spirit.

And, as we traded our saddles for a seat in the bus, which sped us back to Santa Fe through Sunday traffic, I couldn't help wondering, "Which was real? The past twelve days, which already seemed a dream? Or the civilization to which we were returning?" I myself could remain in Santa Fe, where each day I might look up at the Sangre de Cristos and know what lies behind; but to those who boarded trains and planes for New York, Chicago, and Los Angeles—truly to them those twelve days in the wilderness of the high country must always be an interlude set apart—above—entirely out of this world.

That trail ride brought me two lifelong friends—Terry and Ethel. They were two more examples of how the Land of Enchantment affects visitors. Five months after the ride Terry quit her job in Chicago and returned to Santa Fe. I helped her find a snug apartment tucked away behind a Canyon Road home at the end of a little lane, where she lived until Ethel arrived, who also decided she had to live in Santa Fe.

Terry had kept in touch with Ethel in New York, who told me that her interest in moving to Santa Fe started with a letter from Terry, in which she described how here it was even pleasurable to go out and empty the garbage in the beautiful sunsets. Ethel said, "I'd wanted to pack into the mountains again but didn't have the money; so I wrote Doug O'Bannon at Mountain View Ranch and offered to hire on as kitchen help and whatever else I could do. When he wrote back and agreed, I decided that this was it! I hated New York City, and I'd have Terry as a roommate."

By the time Ethel arrived, Terry had moved to an apartment at 215 Delgado Street, which she described as a large garage remodeled into a cute little place with one bedroom, saying they would alternate sleeping on the sofa bed in the living room.

Ethel later moved to Tesuque just before I left Santa Fe. She accepted a few odds and ends from me, saying she loved the distinctive Mexican leather chairs, and that the huge hip-high box with a large square of wood on top (which was actually a Detour or Stop road sign) had turned into a great table. In addition, she had borrowed a bed from the neighbors and purchased a day bed for the living room as a sofa. It was minimal, but she loved it.

In fact, she loved it so much she asked her landlord about buying it but was told he wished to keep it in the family. Later, Ethel remarked, "I had no idea of the cost of the property at that time, and probably would have talked myself out of it had it been available; but I wish I had known then what I know now. I would have begged, borrowed or—well, maybe not stolen—to buy it. Tesuque has become a bedroom community for some of the rich and famous—Hollywood celebrities and English dukes with gated estates. I can't even imagine what that property I rented is worth now. I paid $65 a month rent."

Both Ethel and Terry had come when I was at the Chamber of Commerce, had later married, had children, and still live in Santa Fe and love it. I fully understood why they loved the area, and expressed this in an early greeting I sent out for Thanksgiving Day of 1954, along with a long list of things I was thankful for:

> . . . this fabulous New Mexico with its perfect climate of brilliant blue skies and sunshine that defies you to be down for long . . . a land of manana with a flavor of antiquity, where one is not crushed by the weight of boredom or extravagant living . . . where one feels the strengths of nature in beauties and austerities softened by colors so subtle they get down deep inside and stay there. You come to know New Mexico has a philosophy all its own, and you're a part of it. Like each time I think of all this I sometimes have stopped to say to myself, "And I live here!"

A memorable part of working at the Chamber of Commerce was the people who were part of our "family." Buck Riordan, the TWA representative from Albuquerque who helped so much with the Resort Roundup, visited us regularly with news from the big city to the south. Bespectacled chamber member Ned Gold was another regular part of our family, whom I have periodically remembered over the years each time I use a Sunbeam toaster he told me to buy. And there was our beloved Phil Higgins, business editor of the daily *New Mexican,* who wrote "Peak of the Week" in verse, which appeared on page one of the Sunday edition.

One activity members of the Chamber of Commerce enjoyed was working with movie producers when they shot films around Santa Fe. Together we would advertise and hire numerous locals for movie extras, and even scout doubles for the stars.

The first movie I saw made was *Two Flags West,* starring Joseph Cotton and Linda Darnell. Handsome Jeff Chandler was also in the cast. We helped the producer negotiate with the Indians since the film crew actually wanted to take over Tesuque Pueblo. For this western the pueblo was made over into a small adobe fort with military personnel. The Tesuque Indians were paid several hundred dollars a day for the use of their pueblo, and Columbia Pictures installed a septic tank system, put electrical wires underground, and built little portals (open porches) on some of the adobe houses, which the Indians liked.

My experience of watching the filming of *Two Flags West* contributed to my disillusionment with movies because I saw how they faked things that look real in the final picture. While watching, we were also amazed at how many times they filmed takes—even repeatedly burning covered wagons and buildings. When the wagons were set on fire, the wood was somehow treated so just the cloth tops would burn. To burn buildings, they built corrugated metal housing that enclosed gas jets behind a window in an adobe wall. These jets could be lit so flames poured out or turned off to stop the flames. And many fadeouts were forever spoiled for me as I saw the tracks they had build for cameras to follow the loving couple as they disappeared into the sunset during the finale. I wrote to family and friends telling about another movie that was filmed in Santa Fe in October of 1954:

> Watch for the Columbia picture *Man from Laramie* with Jimmy Stewart, on account of it was filmed on several locations right around Santa Fe. It's special 'cause it was Jimmy's fiftieth picture! The cast includes Kathy O'Donnel, Aileen McMahon, Donald Crisp, George Kennedy, and Ford somebody—I can't recall his first name.
>
> They built a beautiful big ranch house and all the outbuildings—corral, windmill, blacksmith shop, etc., under a couple of huge spreading cottonwood trees some miles south of here, near where the Santa Fe train comes in at Lamy. I should say they built the facades. The adobe part was formed out of some kind of asbestos stuff to make a big house shell in front, was held up by a kind of scaffolding in the back. In the picture it surely does give you the impression of a good solid building.
>
> Then, after they moved to Tesuque Pueblo, about six miles north of town, they made the pueblo into a little town with blacksmith shop, hotel, general merchandise, feed store, sheriff's office, which had all the "Wanted" signs on the wall. There was a big corral in the center of the plaza.
>
> A week ago Terry and I went out to watch them film. It turned out to be a big celebration and commemoration of Jimmy Stewart's fiftieth picture. As we came in, they were filming a fight scene. A villain in fancy black leather westerns was just climbing out of a horse trough as Jimmy hits him again and knocks him back, just as a gang rides up on horses and starts a fight with Jimmy. For that they used his double; but it actually was the day I got to speak with him. He said he loved our country and would like to come back sometime.
>
> I have several shots taken right beside the big camera, about six feet from Jimmy. The camera guys were great,

even telling us how to set our own! As I said, they do a shot over and over again. The camera was right behind the trough, and as they were trying it again, the director yelled at the guy, "This time get your ass down closer to the water . . . you're splashing the lens!" Then he turned, seeing we ladies, and went on with a sheepish grin.

When they finished the sequence, it was lunch time. Because of the celebration we were all invited and got in the chow line for a ham lunch, along with all the extra Indians, Mexicans, and the stars. We got our plates filled and ate with Donald Crisp, who invited us to share his table—a big crate that had held a huge bottle. He told us some of the cast were getting sick from the water, so they were sending it in from Hollywood. He willingly posed for pictures, and we also got a posed shot of War Eagle, a real Indian they'd brought from Hollywood for speaking parts.

When lunch was over, we all gathered in the plaza, where they had a huge three-tiered cake on a big table with MAN FROM LARAMIE in frosting on the side, and a foot-high "50" on top. There were about twenty camera men, plus all we amateurs taking shots with different groupings of the Indians as the cake was cut. Then the Tesuque tribe went through an elaborate ceremony, taking Jimmy in as a member. Wish I could remember his Indian name, but translated it means "Tall Aspen Mountain."

Then they all did the Deer Dance and the Buffalo Dance for him, with camera men herding them around so they could get pictures with the cast in the background. We all had a piece of cake! It's really wonderful how they treat sightseers—almost as guests. I suppose they think that if we're happy we'll tell our friends to be sure to see the picture, as I'm doing! Jimmy's wife was there, too. She's an attractive, tall dark brunette quite striking in neat plaid shorts and bright red knee socks. Seems like a great person.

They started filming again, with Aileen riding in on a buggy, stopping, and with rifle in hand threatening to shoot off a guy's thumb if he didn't do what she said.

Then another fight. There are doubles for the leads to do
the dirty work; and it's really funny to see Jimmy Stewart
talking to Jimmy Stewart. The stand-in looked a lot like
him, was the same build, and of course was dressed the
same. It was hard to tell them apart.

In this fight the guys were supposed to knock each
other through the corral fence; so a prop man came out
with his little saw and cut neat V's in the back so it
wouldn't show, but the fence would break easily and
clean. The other guys had the job of moving the cattle
around the corral as they were needed in the background.
Two others hid among the cattle with a compressed air
tank and hose to make "dust!"

There are scads of Indian and Spanish extras who stand
around in colorful costume. They get moved so as to
look casual in the picture. Understand they get $10 a day,
and even the cattle get so much/head/day if they're in
the picture, and another figure if they're just standing by.
The whole crew stays at La Fonda Hotel right across
from the Chamber, and are constantly in the lobby and
around town. There's also a call board in the lobby telling
where and when they're filming, who's to be on the set,
etc., so it's easy to tell just where to go. I think it's to be
in Technicolor and with some kind of wide-angle screen,
so it should be worth seeing. It will give you an idea of
some of the country around here.

I had a lot of comments from family and friends I had told
about the picture; for of course we all loved Jimmy Stewart,
and this experience did make watching him in other films more
fun because I had actually met him.

A year or so later they were filming *Cowboy* with Glenn Ford
and Jack Lemmon along the Rio Grande north of town. Ethel
and I drove out to watch late one morning. Although that day
the sun was beating down and the filming was out among the
low piñon trees with no shade, we were fascinated with how
they filmed short sequences of action, which had to be connected later to make the film. We talked with a woman whose

job it was to make sure the actor who was wearing a red kerchief as they quit filming that sequence was wearing the same kerchief when they continued next time.

Up near the big canteen bus there were huge urns of what seemed to be iced tea. Since we were very thirsty in the hot weather and there were not too many spectators about, I said to Ethel, "I'll bet they wouldn't mind if we snitched a cup." We thought we had been caught as a man walked up to us. But, instead of mentioning the tea, he said, "Have you had lunch?" Since we had not, he added, "I'll see what I can do. We had half a fried chicken, and they usually make just enough." Soon, however, he returned carrying two plates with half a chicken on each, plus all the trimmings. He joined us at a long table, where we had a great chat, learning they had brought up herds of Mexican longhorn cattle for the film. At one point he disappeared and returned with apple pie and a pint of half-and-half to pour on top.

We later felt for the cattle as we watched the crew trying to produce a stampede, rattling strings of cans and using gunshot. We did not get a very good impression of Glenn Ford, whom we watched come swishing down a long hillside on his horse over and over again. However, we had an unusual opportunity to meet Jack Lemmon and his son, who was about eight. We were sitting on the opposite hillside watching Ford, and had an interesting discussion between takes. Lemmon loved New Mexico and said he would like to come back sometime to explore more of it. And I could see this was an especially fun time because he could have his son with him, who knew a lot about horses. It was fun listening to their comments about Glenn Ford's riding and wondering what they would say to him later. I felt Lemmon was undoubtedly as great a dad as he's been the actor so many people have enjoyed over the years.

Santa Fe also had a resident movie star—Greer Garson. If you saw her on the street, it was likely you would not even recognize the redhead in casual clothes. She and her husband

Buddy Fogelson had a ranch nearby, and each left their mark in Santa Fe. Greer will be remembered for the Greer Garson Theatre at the College of Santa Fe; and Buddy gave a piece of land to the Unitarians in Santa Fe as a location for the church they intended to build. They later got permission to sell the land and purchase a lovely adobe church from the Mormons on Barcelona at Galisteo, where Fellowship Hall is named for Fogelson.

During all the years I worked at the Chamber of Commerce as office manager, I felt fortunate to be learning so much about New Mexican history and culture at a time when most women still did not have jobs outside the home—even though I still feel some guilt in contributing to the eventual development of Santa Fe as a major tourist center and popular place to live.

CHAPTER 6

LOS ALAMOS – WARTIME and PEACETIME

Shortly after I arrived in Santa Fe, I was excited to learn that Martha, an old friend, was the wife of Don MacMillan, one of the top physicists at Los Alamos who had worked on what was referred to up there as "the gadget"—the first atomic bomb. Martha and I had been roommates in the hospital at Stuttgart when we both had broken bones during the occupation days of World War II. Don looked exactly like a scientist—tall, lanky, and bespectacled. Off-duty he was a devoted modern music fan, and a whole bank of dials covered the walls of their extra bedroom.

On Christmas 1949, I was invited to a Los Alamos party at Martha and Don's. The house was filled with atomic scientists, drinks in hand, chatting and comparing their collections of early science fiction. Don related the scenario of a science fiction yarn he wanted Martha to write, and added, "You know, the first country that gets a satellite will have the world by the tail." As I heard these words, I was aghast and thought to myself, "Gosh, how far out can you crazy scientists be!" How could I even imagine that one day we would be worried about the traffic pattern in space.

Some months later, Jack Hodges, a tall Texan with chiseled features, was to become my most important link to activities at Los Alamos. He always looked crisp and clean with a neat haircut—not the casual type so common in Santa Fe. I had met Jack through friends when he was at the New Mexico School of Mines at Socorro, a small town over sixty miles south of Albuquerque and about 125 miles from Santa Fe.

Jack would drive up to Santa Fe to see me, and two or three times I drove down to spend the weekend in Socorro. We were often joined by his special friends Hart and Marg Miller for trips into the mountains. I had also accepted an invitation to join the two on a trip to Aspen, Colorado, over the Christmas holidays. In 1952, Jack moved to Los Alamos as a physicist to work under J. Robert Oppenheimer, director of Los Alamos National Laboratory.

Oppenheimer had gone to the Los Alamos Boys School on the Parajita Plateau across the Rio Grande from Santa Fe. Later, he remembered the isolation he had experienced there; and since the early atomic research was a top secret operation, he nostalgically selected it as a spot to work on the first atomic bomb, and the Manhattan Project was moved to Los Alamos.

With an address of P.O. Box 1663, Santa Fe, New Mexico, in early days Los Alamos could be reached only by a nondescript dirt road coming in from the north, which led to the buildings of the old private school named Los Alamos after the cottonwood trees.

Santa Fe citizens knew nothing about it. Those who worked there were forbidden to discuss anything—even to use the word *physicist*. Telephone calls were monitored. Ingoing and outgoing mail was censored, and it was illegal to mail a letter except in the authorized drops. Driving licenses were all made out with fictitious names, men's names were changed (Fermi became Farmer), and in wedding ceremonies only first names were used. I had heard that men could bring their families, but the family could not leave once they arrived. The scientists working there spoke of the "gadget"—the bomb that was to change our world in ways we still cannot comprehend.

I learned many facts about Los Alamos from my Santa Fe friend Foster Hyatt, who worked for architect Willard Kruger in his Santa Fe offices at Sena Plaza just across from the Post Office. Willard Kruger was one of the architects involved in creating the buildings at Los Alamos. Foster told me about the fascinating history of Sena Plaza, near the place where all Los Alamos scientists reported, and how it happened to become that charming spot of downtown Santa Fe.

An old Santa Fe friend told Helen, his wife, how in the 1800s it became the center for the upper-class Spanish through the hospitality of Doña Isabel and Don José Sena. It began when Don José inherited a small house on a huge land grant just north of the cathedral.

They had eleven children, and, as the Spanish did, they kept building on to that tiny house until it had thirty-three rooms on the south, east, and west sides of a big courtyard. The servants, horses, and chickens were in separate buildings on the north in one-story adobes, except on the west, where they built an outside stairway that led to a large ballroom. They said that room was large enough to hold the legislative assembly one time when the capitol burned in 1892. The second stories (the ones we see today) were added in the 1920s. That's where the Willard Kruger offices were.

When I mentioned to Foster that I had gone to an office in another little courtyard when I applied for my job at Los Alamos, he said, "Oh yes, that's Trujillo Plaza at 109 Palace Avenue. That was the Santa Fe location where all the Los Alamos scientists first reported for duty and got their mail, which came addressed P.O. Box 1663, Santa Fe, Mew Mexico.

"People in Santa Fe knew nothing about the secret road that led to the labs of top physicists of the world, whose names we all know today—J. Robert Oppenheimer, Hans Bethe, Edward Teller, and young Richard Feynman. In addition, many visiting scientists came to help—such as Enrico Fermi, I. I. Rabi, John von Neumann, and Niels Bohr—all working with stuff we'd never heard about, like fission, cross sections, and spherical imploding shock waves."

Foster said he wondered "about the Indians at San Ildefonso way back then, since the secret road went nearby their pueblo. They knew it went up to that boys' school; but they must have wondered when all those trucks kept going by with big stuff to build all we did up there. I understand they did hire some of the men at San Ildefonso Pueblo, but if they did, I wondered what they'd been told."

Then I asked Foster more about the Kruger crew who had
been part of the Manhattan Project, the huge organization of
architects and engineers involved in the creation of buildings at
Los Alamos. He replied, "They were a good bunch to work
with. Some came from Michigan and New York. They'd never
heard of New Mexico and thought they should get out-of-
country pay!" Later, in a note he described the difficulties of
designing buildings for something that had never been done
before or thought possible—even by some of the scientists:

> The road to Los Alamos was a primitive dirt one. One
> time going to The Hill on a winter Monday morning,
> Bob was driving the Kruger station wagon. We hit some
> ice and slid to within a few feet of an unprotected hun-
> dred-foot drop-off just before we got to the top and
> drove under the manned machine guns at the check
> point.
> In the early days of Los Alamos, I was in the crew draft-
> ing on location. If it was necessary to leave your table for
> an hour, when you came back it would be so covered
> with dirt you couldn't see the line work. Many of the
> Army engineers supervising us were as ignorant of what
> they were supposed to be doing as we were. A huge guy
> named Tiny was one of my favorite practicing engineers
> on the project. After a session with the Army engineers,
> he said, "The only thing about them is they mistake a
> state of confusion for progress."
> The physicists' heads too were filled with figures that
> meant nothing to us; and they had no idea what they
> needed in the way of a building to work in. Many of the
> structures appeared to be observation posts for monitor-
> ing heavy explosions; so our practice was to use six feet of
> concrete with all the reinforcing justified and cover it
> with two or three feet of dirt.
> Matt, one of our field supervisors came in and men-
> tioned an underground structure in which I had called
> for two feet of dirt to be placed over heavy log beams, for
> after the war we were not allowed to use steel. Matt

checked the design and asked, "Did you intend the dirt
to be put on with a bulldozer?" I shot back, "Hell no!"
"Well they did, and it didn't cave in." This gives you
some idea of those crazy days. It was amazing how many
who came from the East remained in Santa Fe following
the war. Like Helen and I, they couldn't be driven away.
 Well that hidden project up on the plateau under the
cottonwoods grew to a community of 15,000. We still
had to have a pass at the gate to enter that someone up
there had arranged for; but there was a lovely highway up
to The Hill as we called it.

The Santa Fe Chamber of Commerce had not been successful in attracting the Atomic Energy Commission offices when
they were moved from Los Alamos—a fact that perhaps helped
keep population growth from exploding until recently.
Albuquerque was chosen instead, and Sandia Base and
Laboratories had also been established there in 1940 when
there was a population of 35,550. As a result, by 1950 the population of Albuquerque had grown to nearly 100,000 and was
close to 300,000 in the early 1990s.
 On July 16, 1995, we celebrated the fiftieth anniversary of
the world's first atomic explosion, and in the many articles
written, we learned more about the secret activities on The
Hill. The whole operation had been code-named Trinity by the
physicists, who were not even sure it was going to work.
 When the first plutonium bomb was detonated at 5:29:45
atop a 100-foot tower at Alamogordo Army Air Base in the
New Mexican desert, its power far surpassed expectations as it
produced a mushroom cloud higher than Mt. Everest. The
estimated force of that first atomic blast was between 20,000
and 22,000 tons of TNT, which left a 500-foot-wide crater,
completely vaporizing the steel tower. Desert sand was fused to
glass within an 800-yard radius beneath the mushroom cloud,
which rose to 40,000 feet. The first official news report to the
public stated that an ammunition dump had blown up.
 Leading designer J. Robert Oppenheimer stood aghast,

sometime later uttering words of an Indian sacred text: "I am become Death—the shatterer of worlds." Later, British Prime Minister Winston Churchill used a biblical exclamation to describe the event: "This is the Second Coming, in wrath!"

The bomb had been built in the hope of using it to end World War II, which it did four weeks later. Japan surrendered after two of these innovations had exploded over Hiroshima and Nagasaki. Robert Lewis, copilot of Enola Gay, the plane that dropped the bomb, said, "My God, what have we done!"

Another more humanistic part of the Los Alamos story involves a woman named Edith Warner, who left Philadelphia in the 1920s when she was thirty to come to New Mexico for her health. When her money ran out, she took a job accepting mail and storing supplies left by the narrow gauge Chili Line railway at the Otowi Bridge stop for the Los Alamos School for Boys further up the hill. She rented a nearby rundown house from the family of Maria Martinez, world-famous San Ildefonso potter who made the first distinctive black pieces. Historically, the place was known as "the house at Otowi Bridge."

Edith found a mystical union with her San Ildefonso friends —a shared understanding of nature that made her quick to respond to wisdoms of personal union with their nature gods. In fact, she became so much a part of their community that they helped her remodel the little house into a store and restaurant, which provided a small income from passersby and boys from the Los Alamos school who came down to swim in the river.

Then in the 1940s Edith found herself living beside a bridge that spanned two worlds. This woman, who had left civilization in the East for the solitude of New Mexico, became part of a secret society of scientists and their families from around the world. In her house at Otowi Bridge, she became a lifesaving presence for Manhattan Project scientists who were secretly pushing to save our world from destruction. Not all strangers,

LEFT: Indians at the Intertribal Indian Ceremonial.

BELOW: Dance at the Gallup Intertribal Indian Ceremonial, attended by President Eisenhower.

ABOVE: Looking down East San Francisco Street toward St. Francis Cathedral, La Fonda Hotel on right. BELOW: Spectators line the roofs of La Fonda Hotel during Fiesta.

Brochure for La Fonda Hotel, circa 1950.

Program cover for the first Santa Fe Opera.

The picturesque patio of Foster and Helen Hayatts 250-year-old adobe on Canyon Road.

The Original Curio Store, which housed Walt and Alma Wright's rock shop. Today it still looks much the same as it did in 1952.

The author and Ethel on a rockhounding expedition.

La Fonda Hotel circa 1953 decked out with *farolitos* and other Christmas decorations.

she had known the civilian director of the project, J. Robert Oppenheimer, since 1937, when he had been a student at the Los Alamos school.

Like her Indian friends, Edith was a model of discretion in these secretive times. Every evening, one and sometimes two groups of overworked, tension-filled men and their families from The Hill would come to her place for dinner and to relax with the smell of piñon wood burning in a corner fireplace, often socializing around candlelit tables. Her menus featured a simple stew flavored with herbs served on huge colorful Mexican plates, posole, an Indian dish made of parched corn, lettuce in a black pottery bowl, freshly baked bread, a sweet tomato relish, watermelon pickle, spiced peaches or apricots, and a dessert of raspberries.

Although Edith was loved and admired by all, she had a special relationship with Danish Nobel Prize winner Niels Bohr, who is known today for his theory of complementarity, a way of regarding light as composed either of waves or of particles. His theory, which seems to mean that harmony in nature is a kind of interplay of apparently conflicting forces, could have a strong impact on the way we perceive the world and ourselves.

I was fascinated with this concept, for it could explain the close relationship between Warner and Bohr in connection to her unusual acceptance by Indian friends. She never asked what their ceremonies meant—she seemed to know. And this knowing was something her San Ildefonso friends had always experienced, the dual nature of life which reveals itself in contrasting relationships—earth and sky, summer and winter, male and female—within nature's harmony.

Edith Warner's Pueblo Indian friends believed that this earth we live on is sacred—each stone and bush and tree alive with a spirit of life like their own. Their sun god brings night and day, leans down in the form of clouds, and walks the earth embodied in the shape of rain and rainbows. They know that the harmony of our world depends on us; and that it is our duty to maintain this harmony by the way we live—something we're learning the hard way. The maintenance of such harmony necessitates a return to the importance of togetherness in family and community, not only as human beings, but in connection with our earth and sky, our plants and animals. And Niels Bohr also spoke out about these special relationships. He said in an open letter to the United Nations:

> An open world where each nation can assert itself solely to the extent to which it can contribute to the common culture and is able to help others with experience and resources must be the goal to be put before everything else. . . . The development of technology has now reached a stage where the facilities for communication have provided the means for making all mankind a cooperating unity . . . at the same time fatal consequences to civilization may ensue unless international divergences are considered as issues to be settled by consultation based on free access to all relevant information.[*]

After the war atomic research continued at Los Alamos, contributing to the increased population on The Hill. The narrow-gauge railroad tracks were torn up, and the old road had to be replaced. In 1946, Edith Warner learned that plans for a new bridge would bring traffic into her yard almost beneath her kitchen window. Consequently, many members of the Los Alamos and San Ildefonso communities volunteered to help her. No one really knew how it started, but more than fifteen young physicists who had been part of the birth of the bomb, and wives who had shared long months of tension before the test explosion and had come to her for eggs, fresh fruits, and vegetables, began to work side by side with men and women from San Ildefonso to help build a new home for Warner. It become a truly community affair, with more and more volunteers wishing to help.

---

[*] Peggy Pond Church, *The House at Otowi Bridge* (Albuquerque: University of New Mexico Press, 1959, 1960), 94.

An Indian from the pueblo made adobes and acted as boss, sometimes frustrating scientists, who would find that during the week the Indians would change what the physicists had done on weekends. But the Indians seemed to have an inate know-how. Often grandfatherly, they would say, "This is the way we do it," or "No, not that way, this way." As a result, the project was an extension of the cooperation between people of the area that had existed during the Manhattan Project.

When Edith Warner died in 1951, Niels Bohr wrote her sister, acknowledging Edith's important role as a unifying force:

> The memory of Edith Warner, a noble personality, and of the enchanting environment in which she lived, will always be cherished by everyone who met her. Although in the days of the war it was not possible to speak freely about the hopes and anxieties in one's mind, I felt that your sister had an intuitive understanding which was a bond between us.[*]

At the time the bomb was dropped, I was not immediately aware of the fear it had created in people until I read an article using the word *futurelessness*. Then in the 1950s we were indoctrinated with the need for air raid shelters. I remember a 400-page Federal Civil Defense Administration bulletin (third edition, 1955) that specified actions to be taken in case of nuclear attack.

HOME PROTECTION EXERCISES
(Family Action Program):

1. What to Do When the Signals Sound
2. Preparation of Your Shelter
3. Home Fire Prevention
4. Home Fire Fighting
5. Emergency Action to Save Lives

---

[*] Peggy Pond Church, *The House at Otowi Bridge* (Albuquerque: University of New Mexico Press, 1959, 1960).

6. What to Do If Someone Is Trapped
7. Provision of Safe Food and Water in Emergencies
8. Home Nursing.

Another Civil Defense technical bulletin dated May 1958 said that since the intensity of fallout at any specific place in the United States was impossible to predict, it might require staying in a shelter two or more weeks.

That year at Christmas I received a hand-printed card saying,"Greetings from Tomatzu's Fallout Shelter." Beside Louise and Chuzo's note were their oriental signatures and a picture of a character with a big hat struggling under a wide umbrella with pants and shirt pinned on and hanging down the sides—all under a huge mushroom cloud. Their artwork added a bit of wry humor to a sobering situation.

Chuzo was a Japanese artist who had come to Santa Fe with his American wife Louise sometime in the 1940s. In addition to other artwork, he made portraits, and according to my friend Ethel, once did a pastel of her and friends in a dance class and gave it to them. Chuzo's wife Louise still runs a gallery, where there must be hundreds of his works.

Secrecy was still a part of Los Alamos life in the 1950s. I never knew what Jack did as a physicist except that he worked under Don MacMillan. And since it was still a closed community, any trip I made to The Hill involved preplanning. Jack would have to request a pass that would be ready at the gate. Sometimes we ate at his apartment, and often visited other Los Alamos friends for an evening. A lovely winding mountain road had been built to the historic community of scientific laboratories and exciting homesites on a long finger mesa of the Jemez Mountains extending out into the Rio Grande Valley.

From the original shacks, the laboratories spread out, replacing what would ordinarily have been a downtown commercial section in other communities. This contributed to the still artificial kind of living that sent most of the Los Alamos workers to Santa Fe for shopping and entertainment, often spending so much time in Santa Fe it seemed they were like suburbanites coming downtown. And for most Santa Feans in the 1950s who did not have friends on The Hill to visit, Los Alamos was just another town in the vicinity.

Jack came down to Santa Fe a couple of times a week, often for meals. Although he felt I was a pretty good cook, as a southerner there were two things he kept harping about—corn bread and grits. My corn bread was only politely appreciated, but I kept trying. Once at a dinner party at friends the hostess had some which was thin and chewy. I got the recipe, which had just enough white flour to bind the cornmeal together, and smugly tried it on Jack. He was in seventh heaven—ate it with the meal, had it with cream and sugar for dessert, and took home what was left for his breakfast. However, I never did master the art of cooking grits to Jack's satisfaction.

Jack and I often ate out. One favorite spot was the Pink Adobe on College Street, which touted a New Orleans atmosphere. There was an outdoor patio and several indoor home-like rooms. Tables and seating arrangements were individually unique, some built in along walls with tables and seats of every size and shape. I recall the time I ordered a drippy green chile dish while sitting against the wall behind our table, which was a low piano bench beneath our knees.

Green chile was my favorite; and I learned how to roast and peel them for a special soup recipe I had. But I, like most visitors to the area, enjoyed seeing *ristras*—strings of fat red chiles hanging out to dry. I discovered that chile hotness depended on the variety and the soil in which it was grown. Some restaurants catering to tourists labeled their chile dishes hot, medium, or mild; and it seemed that native Santa Feans loved the hottest variety. I often wondered whether their taste buds were conditioned to the point where they no longer could enjoy milder seasonings.

Jack was not a chile fan, ever searching for something more sophisticated on a menu. I recall being chastised for not appreciating exotic wild rice as we ate at Sagebrush Inn in Taos. We also ate at La Cozina de Taos, an intimate restaurant near the Plaza.

I was amused that restaurants and motels in Taos would say in their advertising "Home of Kit Carson" or "Kit Carson slept here." However, after reading about Kit Carson's life, I learned impressive facts about a man I'd known only by name; he was a mountain man, trapper, hunter, scout, linguist, colonel, and counselor between Indians and whites. Indian Agent General Sherman said of him, "These Red Skins think Kit twice as big a man as me . . . they would believe him and trust him any day before me."

During this time Jack taught me much about photography, once advising me to stop taking pictures of people unless they were truly part of a larger scene. I recall one aspen season as we were driving slowly through a golden wooded area. In front of us in the road was a mother skunk followed by three darling baby skunks. Jack stopped the car and pulled me back after I had thrown open the door to get out and take a picture, reminding me why it was best to just sit still and watch.

Another fall at the height of the aspen season, Jack and I saw notices in the *New Mexican* that the narrow gauge railway from Chama, New Mexico, to Durango, Colorado, was to be discontinued. We decided to make that last historic trip, driving about eighty miles north in the Jemez Mountains to Chama, where we left our car.

The train trip to Durango turned out to be an unforgettable adventure. The narrow gauge railway was like a big toy train, seemingly built for sightseeing and socializing. Coaches did not have the usual individual installed seats facing forward, but upholstered couch-like seats along the sides. Jack had wrangled special reserved seats for us in the Observation Car, which was carpeted and had individual anchored overstuffed swivel chairs, with an open, railed observation platform at the end of the train.

Since the trip up over Cumbres Pass was slow because of the grade, we had lots of time to spend glued to the windows, exclaiming at the panorama of mountainsides covered with golden aspens. Jack and other photographers hung off the observation platform shooting pictures much of the way. At the highest point, we stopped so passengers could get off to view a breathtaking canyon. Later at dusk, the conductor came back to announce that something was wrong with the generator.

As darkness fell, the only light for our car was a tiny battery lamp about the size of a large flashlight shining down from the ceiling at the rear. At the other end of the Observation Car, was a small enclosure with a table for four, which turned out to be the diner for the train. When another couple went to sit down, Jack said, "Let's try it, too. Maybe they will serve us something." And indeed the cook in the small galley did bring us a steak dinner with cherry pie a la mode. So we could see while we ate, the brakeman set his lantern on the table and joined in the conversation.

When he learned I worked at the Santa Fe Chamber of Commerce he mentioned how much he wished we could bring in more visitors so they could keep the train running, where he'd been brakeman for fifteen years. Then he reminisced about the past. "I suppose it's because most everybody has a car today, and it's not like the old days when for many the train was the only way to get some places. And people weren't in such a hurry. Why I remember when we had more schedules— one that started early in the morning and returned the same day. There were three different men who loved to fish. We'd stop the train to drop them off at a special river, or spots they liked, and stop to pick them up again on the return trip." Jack and I were glad we had had the opportunity to experience that last run of the old narrow gauge. We spent the night in a small hotel in Durango and returned to Santa Fe the next day.

Later that fall, a big change occurred in my Santa Fe life. One day Stella Chavez, a Spanish friend who worked for an architect, called me to join her for a coffee break. When we were seated, she said, "The reason I called is to ask you something. Jesus [her husband] and I have been thinking of leaving Santa Fe for some time, and now we've made the decision. We'll be leaving in November. I told Kenneth I'm quitting,Vi, and he needs someone like you." Kenneth S. Clark was the principal of an architectural firm where Stella worked. I thought for a moment and said, "I have two brothers in the architectural game. I'm not sure I want to be the third one in the family." Stella replied, "But Vi, it won't hurt to talk with him." So I agreed and made an appointment.

As I thought about it, I remembered how often I had said that a two-week vacation just was not enough time out of a whole year. Then I realized that if I decided to make the change, I could resign my position at the Chamber of Commerce in August and have more than two months before going to work for Kenneth Clark—and that is what I finally did.

It was a busy August, making plans for an extensive train trip along the West Coast from Los Angeles up to Portland via Santa Barbara and Berkeley to see college, World War II, and Red Cross friends; and then across to Minnesota and Chicago to visit family. I loved seeing the country on the ground with an old-fashioned railway luxury that Amtrak never could replace.

When my departure date arrived, Jack drove me the twenty miles to Lamy, where I boarded the Atchison, Topeka and Santa Fe Railroad. After I returned, I wrote family and friends, describing the trip in verse:

> Those two whole months of seeing you—my wartime
>   friends and kin,
> Made me feel really ready for work harnessing again!
> And even though my working for an architect makes
>   three,
> It's worth my giving it a try, and in a year we'll see!
>
> My office is shiny and pleasant; my boss is a
>   wonderful guy
> The drafting room guys crazy screwballs
>   and there we see eye to eye!

So in job and in home I'm all settled, with a winter
   of skiing ahead,
And with prospects of Aspen for Christmas, it's just
   as I always have said . . .
I'm a pretty lucky gal!

The ski trip to Aspen, Colorado, did come off. I started my
brand-new job in November, and then asked for a week's vacation over Christmas and New Year's and got it! I was excited
to try the new ski operation that had just opened in Aspen.
Jack was no skier so didn't go, and was unhappy that I'd be
away for the holidays. I'd kept in touch with Hart and Marg
Miller (Jack's friends in Socorro), who had been checking out
the touted new ski area at Aspen. They sent a colorful brochure
I poured over, which said,

> Aspen in the Roaring Fork Valley of the Colorado
> Rockies is singularly blessed with a long season of deep
> powder snow and winter sunshine. Aspen winters are
> warm and particularly sunny with ordinarily very little wind.
> Aspen offers the widest possible accommodations for
> skiers. The Hotel Jerome is the gathering place for all.
> Rich in background, the Jerome combines Victorian
> atmosphere and modern comfort with hospitality of the
> old West—tea in the Blue Lounge, cocktails in the
> Frontiersman's Bar and dinner in the attractive dining
> room where the best of Swiss cuisine is served. Rooms,
> including meals, $9.00 to $15.00 double occupancy.
> While dogs are not permitted in any hotel properties,
> kennels are available at Glenwood Springs.
> Ski lift, a single ride, $2.20; a daily ticket, $4.00; three-
> day ticket, $10.90. A daily T-bar lift ticket, $2.80. For the
> ski-school, half-day $3.50, day, $4.50, 3-day, $12.00, or
> week, $22.00. A private lesson for one, $8.50.

The trip to Aspen was an exciting week. Hart and Marg
picked me up in Santa Fe, and we started north, with nary a
flake of snow on the ground. I'd said on the way, "But Hart,

are you sure we'll be skiing? There's no snow!" Then we stopped for coffee at Pueblo, Colorado, and as we came out, there were flakes in the air. It snowed all the rest of the way. We went the long way around since going through Leadville could be tricky. I'd read stories of wagon loads going off the road, or sinking completely out of sight in bogs of mud.

We stayed at a small lodge not too far from the Purple Onion, one of the special new nightspots. There was a Christmas greeting from the *Aspen Flyer* with notes from other places like The Red Onion, The Tom Thumb, The Pied Piper, The Sun Deck, The Prospector, The Country Store, The Smuggler, and service stations, laundries, and beauty shops. The lifts seemed quite civilized compared to ours at Santa Fe Basin—short lines, and the long slopes were great. We skied most of the day and partied at night.

At lunch one day we ate with a man who was superintendent of schools at Bakersfield, California, and his wife. They said, "We're driving up to Toklat Lodge tomorrow. It's up in the Maroon Bells-Snowmass Wilderness. Would you like to join us?" Of course we would. They told us that the owner of Toklat Wilderness Lodge and Husky Kennels had purchased dogs from the Army, where he'd been a trainer. He and his wife served gourmet dinners at the sprawling mountain lodge and took tourists on dog-sled treks.

It was a crisp winter day with feathery flakes lazing down. From Aspen we drove quite a few miles further up into the mountains in a convertible with the top down! As we arrived at the lodge, we went around back to see nearly sixty Alaskan huskies, each chained to a tree with a dog house nearby. It was so exciting, for they were all straining at the end of their chains in a tail-wagging welcome. We loved it; and as we were exclaiming, an Eskimo man who worked there said, "Would you like to hear them sing?" "Oh yes!" we answered. Then he said something to them in muckluck language, and their noses went up in the air and all at the same time they let out a loud, long "whooooooooo," an almost bloodcurdling song. It was unforgettable!

We took the short Husky Tour behind the dogs and returned for dinner beside a roaring fire in the attractive lodge. Although we didn't spend the night, I read about accommodations in the Toklat Lodge brochure: "Lodge rates American Plan, Summer $7.50 to $9.00; Winter $8.50 to $10.00. A dog-sledding trek to the base of Star Peak, two-sled passengers, $12.50 each. To the end of the valley with snow picnic stopover, $15.00 each."

Toward the end of that week it started clouding up and snowed. On Thursday thick fog moved in, and skiing was not only risky but scary, as our skis would drop into space without our being able to see why, only to be slapped back up almost under our chins.

One evening we attended a party at the home of one of the ski instructors, and I was astonished to see Bavarian Tony Woerndle, a ski instructor from Garmisch, where I had been director of the Red Cross Olympic Club after World War II, and where the Winter Olympics had been held in 1936. It was great reminiscing with Tony; and I loved the stories he told as we sat around on the floor guzzling hot mulled wine.

One ski bum whose gang had gone to the California coast during the summer said they tried to live off the land and sea. Then they heard of a pet store where they could buy horse meat that was far cheaper than beef. He said, "We'd go in and say things like, 'Our Pekingese is pretty old, and some of her teeth are gone—do you have a good tender fillet?'"

They were laughing about this one day as a wealthy old man who lived in a mansion up the shore was walking the beach. He stopped to chat and was intrigued with their story about the meat market. Some days later he threw a big dinner party, serving horse meat to his wealthy friends. They seemed to thoroughly enjoy the lovely fillets until he calmly announced what they were eating.

That night it snowed heavily, and by Friday skiing was impossible. Even the streets in Aspen were becoming almost tunnels between the high drifts plowed on either side. Hart and Marg didn't have to get back to Santa Fe, but I did. Thinking I better start, I took the bus to Glenwood Springs. It was still snowing, and I remember electric cables breaking along the way creating big flares. Our bus driver would stop now and then and use a kitchen broom to clear the windshield of snow the wipers couldn't handle.

At the hotel in Glenwood Springs, we learned that no buses had been through in either direction; but I'd planned to take the train, which went down the Royal Gorge. That night they awakened me at the hotel, saying, "Just had a call the Royal Gorge train is canceled; but we think the California Zephyr will be through at 3:30 this afternoon." And since the Zephyr had Vista Domes with extra seats, they sold quite a number of us tickets and said, "If Miller's the conductor, he'll board you all."

He did; and while we wound through the mountains New Year's Eve merriment was building as the announcement came over loudspeakers, "We hope you won't mind if we pick up more stranded skiers at Winter Park." I sat with Ellen, a nurse who worked in Pueblo, Colorado. This meant we'd be trying to take the same train out of Denver, where we had a three-hour layover.

As we waited, Ellen said, "I have a bottle of burgundy in my bag." So we celebrated on a bench in the Denver station, drinking out of the bottle. The Pueblo train was an oldie with a stove at one end of the coach. I spent the night with Ellen at the hospital, and had to get a bus to Santa Fe the next day.

It was a Christmas to remember! My new boss and the guys in the drafting room didn't mind my getting back late after they'd heard my story.

CHAPTER 7

-- --

ARCHITECTS and the ARTS

When I began working as office manager for the architect
Kenneth S. Clark, his office became my second home,
and a crew of wonderful draftsmen my family with whom I had
interesting conversations at coffee breaks.

From my apartment on Canyon Road, I walked to work
across the Santa Fe River bridge and along Castillo, which no
longer exists because Paseo de Peralta has forever changed that
part of old Santa Fe. Then I'd continue straight ahead on
Castillo with St. Michael's School on the left at Alameda, and
further on past the beginnings of the new hospital on the corner of Palace Avenue. Across the street was the Coronado
Building in which Clark had his offices. It was a stately
Territorial-style building set back from Palace Avenue, with a
green lawn on either side of a wide entrance walkway. I'd enter
down a back stairway to the ground floor.

Most of our architectural commissions were from the
United States Army Corps of Engineers, whose offices were in
Albuquerque. We designed hospitals for United States Army
bases in New Mexico and stations sheltering military instru-
mentations, which were scattered around White Sands Proving
Ground. Some of these sites were theodolite stations at locations like Miller's Watch Site. Evidently Miller had lost his
watch there at one time.

One building we designed for Army computers makes it
clear how far we've come in this electronic age. The 1950s
marked the beginning of the computer era. By contrast to the
laptops of today, computers of that time were unbelievably
huge, covering walls of large buildings stories high. In addition, because they were powered by thousands of vacuum

103

tubes, room temperature had to be maintained by large air conditioners.

Some of our consulting engineers came from Albuquerque. I especially remember Frank, our mechanical consultant, for his wise counsel regarding work with the military bureaucracy, "If you're doing work for the Corps of Engineers, you might as well do it their way. You'll save yourselves a lot of time and frustration, ulcers or even your sanity."

Some of our jobs for the Corps of Engineers involved specifications which turned out to be mimeographed books an inch thick. This was my responsibility, which often involved bringing in extra typists and meeting deadlines. We had to type the whole thing with carbon copies to be sent down to Albuquerque for the Corps of Engineers to OK or mark up. Then it was returned for the cutting of mimeograph stencils and production.

Not conditioned to constant repetition, I tried to improve on requirements. Each section started with a long list of related federal specifications that had to be typed: FEDERAL SPECIFICATION B-48-5867 CONCRETE FORMS. I had the women abbreviate to F.S. wherever "federal specification" appeared in these lists, and use other obvious abbreviations which shortened specifications by pages and made for easier reading.

One day Kenneth called me into his office. He pointed to a copy of a first draft we had sent to Albuquerque. On the title page was scrawled in almost illegible handwriting "Your secretary. . . ." Kenneth asked, "What does this mean?" When I admitted what we had done, he said, "Well, Vi, you'd better do it just the way they want it, OK?"

Those were also the days of A. B. Dick mimeograph machines. With our big operations we'd have trouble with paper feed, often when there was a deadline. One time my complaint brought an A. B. Dick vice president to solve our problems. And regarding paper, I remember fondly the salesman for the Santa Fe Book & Stationery who came by each

Monday for an order. He had intrigued us with his story about how he had received $300 for his idea of sticking staples together in strips. He told me, "I was twelve, and Minnesota Mining was selling for ten cents a share; but the least we could buy was $500 worth. I had the $300 in the bank, and begged my dad to lend me $200; but he refused! I've often wondered what one of those ten cent shares of Minnesota Mining might be worth today."

It was during the time I worked for Kenneth Clark that I became interested in nutrition, and the men had to hear about it during coffee breaks. A Santa Fe friend had urged me to read Adelle Davis's *Let's Eat Right to Keep Fit.* I kept putting her off with, "I'm healthy, I don't need anything like this." But she finally wore me down, and once I read the book I was like a new convert to a religion, and started proselytizing.

I became convinced that the medical profession tried to cure us after we were ill but offered no help with disease prevention. In one heavy argument, I quoted from a February 7, 1957, open letter from the Boston Nutrition Society to Dr. Nathan M. Pusey, then president of Harvard University, on the matter of research standards under Dr. Frederick J. Stare, head of the Department of Nutrition at Harvard School of Public Health. One paragraph read:

> Dr. Stare's public utterances, writings and court testimony are all designed to uphold the business status quo by belittling the devastating effects of our denatured "counterfeit" and poisoned foods and by ignoring the increase of degenerative diseases. We can understand this attitude when we read that he received in the past six years $378,000 in gifts largely marked for his personal direction, from the very commercial interests who stand to profit most by keeping our people in ignorance as to the truth about those foods and our national health.

These days, as the price of health care threatens our

national budget, and disease prevention is more in the news, I feel vindicated for all my preaching on the subject. Nutrition wasn't discussed much with the native Spanish, though I felt that with their tortillas and chile they had better nutrition than many of us. At the time I did make some converts among my office family, like the wife of a draftsman who thanked me for learning to feed her children a good healthy breakfast. She told me, "They're not moaning around all morning anymore saying, 'Mom, I'm hungry!'" Interestingly, today Santa Fe has become a center for people focused on nutrition and alternative health care.

That year I sent my usual Christmas greeting in time for Thanksgiving. Part of it said:

I'm still with Kenneth Clark, the architect.
   I never thought I'd be there one whole year;
      But so appreciate the boss and boys
         And working in such a pleasant atmosphere,
         makes every day a pleasure.
We live the casual life—no fuss or strain.
   You go downtown without a hat and glove.
      No mad commuting, pressure, wasting time,
         And that's the kind of living that I love!
The country's stimulating, people too;
   We often "waste" our time discussing things
      In long bull sessions over drink and food
         With all the satisfaction that that brings.

We have our share of characters and more,
      But one thing can be said—they never bore!

How did you like the outcome of the race
   For Prexie of this good old U.S.A.?
      It's all past history now—of this I'm sure —
         It's one we won't forget for many a day.
Let's hope that Ike can make our next year bright,
   And help to make our bank roll not so bent.

At least, now he's elected, I can say
I once had dinner with the President!
Let's hope the faith so many have in him
Will be contagious, and we'll also find
We have more faith in this old world of ours,
And also feel a faith deep down inside,
Each one of us—a faith that better can
Promote the love we should have for our fellow man.

As I wrote this, I thought of the evening I had been a dinner guest in Berlin with Eisenhower. He was most comfortable to be with. Even though he was the commanding general, he was considerate of the GIs, who loved him. In making inspection tours, he'd talk with the men to find out how they were holding up and whether they were getting good food. So I felt as president he would do the same.

When I told him that evening I'd been service club director with the 17th Airborne when they crossed the Rhine, Eisenhower said, "Oh yes. I remember that well. They told me if I went in when I planned to I'd have 90 some percent glider casualties. I knew I had to do it; but I paced the floor the whole night." I thought then how agonizing it must have been for him to make the D-Day decision. No wonder Americans had wanted him to be our president.

I spent that Christmas in Santa Fe. Early in December the whole town was celebrating with lights, and that's when I learned about the proper way to speak of Christmas lighting in New Mexico—the *luminaria-farolito* controversy. Although some would call them *luminarias*, I accepted the idea of *farolitos* being the brown paper bags with tops rolled down and filled with sand to hold candles. When lit, the bags look like big fat candles—rows of which are used to line walkways, homes, or to outline adobe walls. Anyone who has ever spent Christmas in Santa Fe will fondly recall the stunning scene of *farolitos* lining the many-storied parapets of La Fonda.

For me, *luminarias* are the little bonfires usually built along the streets on Christmas Eve—a custom followed in New

Mexico since the time of the first Spanish colonists hundreds of years ago. Some see this as a reenactment of the shepherds' fires which led the way to the stable the night Christ was born. Regardless of which name is correct, I regard both *farolitos* and *luminarias* as a Santa Fe tradition and resent seeing the use of the tradition spread to places like Ohio, Pennsylvania, and even Minnesota.

That year my friends Dave and John, who operated The Centerline Shop, felt we should experience some of the Indian rituals. They said they would drive their big station wagon; so I invited three friends I knew from work.

Of the several Indian pueblos up and down the Rio Grande Valley north and south of Santa Fe, we went first to Tesuque, the nearest pueblo north. Because a priest is customarily at a pueblo on Christmas, the celebration usually includes marriage ceremonies. However, for some reason that year Tesuque was not on the priest's schedule, so we decided to drive south to Santo Domingo, a much larger pueblo with a huge adobe church.

It was a cold, cold night with snow on the ground. Six of us had packed into Dave and John's big station wagon, which had a good heater. As we drove into the pueblo, there was a giant welcoming fire warming the entrance to the big adobe church. We went inside to wait and get out of the wind; but since there were no pews, we had to stand.

After about an hour and a half, the marriage service began with five couples standing up front in a large semicircle facing the priest. Although the Catholic priest used language we did not understand, after some words he symbolically and literally tied each couple together with a big wide sash as he completed the religious service that made them husband and wife.

Following the wedding ceremony, we all left the church to wait for the dancers, who were in their kiva conducting their own secret Christmas ceremonies. We waited and waited, hugging the big fire, which kept us warm on one side at a time as we stomped and turned. It was the largest fire I'd ever seen, built by setting up long branches of wood tepee style, sending flames and sparks high into the dark starry sky.

At one point, Dave and I took a long inspiring stroll through the silent pueblo. We were the only souls walking between the dark adobe homes. Smoke curled up from the many chimneys, carrying our eyes to the jewel-like stars we almost felt we could pick from the midnight sky.

Hours passed. Some took naps in the station wagon; and we were all getting pretty sleepy when finally, just after six in the morning, a long line of dancers came stomping from the kiva through the dark open field into the church. Their bare bodies were covered with black and just a bit of color. Paint mixed with perspiration streaked down their faces beneath feathered headdresses.

The Indian dances I had seen before were unique and colorful; but they had never touched me with their simple dancing and drumming. This time was different. Some elemental part of me resonated with the naked dancers. As I stood within the walls of the church just behind the line of drummers, that elemental feeling increased with intensity until I became a part of the happening in a way I'd never guessed possible.

Later, I recalled what D. H. Lawrence once said after watching naked Indians dancing—that theirs must be a feeling religion. He used words like *inexplicable* and *inscrutable* to describe it. Then I thought of young couples on dance floors with blank stares, gyrating to a primitive rock beat. Was such activity partly the need to return to the more elemental aspects of their being? And once again I wondered how the Indians reconciled all this with their Catholicism. There seemed to be some deep need in all of us to connect with the elemental.

I had a reputation for putting on good parties. New Year's Eve was always at Vi's with friends from work. Refreshments involved hard liquor—tequila for the margaritas and Bacardi rum for the big punch bowls. Our liquor supplies came from one or more annual trips to Juarez across the Mexican border to the South. *Oso Negro* (Black Bear) brand tequila was a

favorite at $.65 a quart—the same which sold for $6.00 to
$7.00 dollars in Santa Fe. We were allowed to bring in a gal-
lon of liquor, often a gallon of Bacardi rum costing under
$5.00. Because we returned to Santa Fe across that tiny tip of
western Texas, we had to add state taxes; but what we saved on
liquor paid for a great long weekend.

Nightclubs in Juarez were inexpensive and fun, with Spanish
music and colorful floor shows. Daytime markets were also
exciting, with interesting glass and pottery that differed from
what I had collected. Bargaining was in vogue for many, but
not for me. If anything, I felt I should pay more than the little
asked for. I bought lovely brown and blue glass that I still love
to use. I find communion and profound expression in the
earthy texture and lack of uniformity of pottery, glass, or tin
made by peasants' hands—far more than in a fragile porcelain
or piece of sparkling crystal.

One New Year's Eve we had fun as we took the yellow tissue off a bottle of Damiana, "The Queen of Liquors" one of
the men had brought to my party. On this tissue it said:

> The well-known and valuable properties of this liquor
> which have been noted by all who have used it, make it
> an inestimable discovery. If taken before meals, it whets
> the appetite. It exerts a wonderful influence upon the
> nervous system, and is a powerful aphrodisiac. The fre-
> quent instances of longevity and the youthful energy pro-
> duced is manifested in both male and female in produc-
> ing offspring. Abuse may result in intoxication; but
> improper use will not result in evil.

In those days there were not the problems with alcohol,
drug abuse, or sexually transmitted diseases we have today.
Although we always had hard liquor at our get-togethers, we
had no problem with drunkenness.

After Christmas and New Year's Santa Feans looked forward
to summer theater each July and August by El Teatro de Santa

Fe. And later, our new Santa Fe Opera became known around the world. The Santa Fe Opera was the brainchild of John O. Crosby, established in the decade following World War II. Crosby had come to love northern New Mexico as a young student at the Los Alamos Ranch School. It is fascinating that attendance by two different persons at the same boys school resulted in Santa Fe's close association with the birthplace of the atomic age and a world-acclaimed opera. This seemed to once again underscore the fact that this was a part of our country that attracts creative souls.

Because of his musical family background, Crosby's military assignments were in the field of music during World War II. While serving in Europe, he became deeply interested in opera. After returning to school in New England following the war, he found opera celebrated largely in big cities of the East. So in thinking of an American opera company, the high, dry climate of New Mexico that he remembered seemed superb. With a loan from his father to realize his dream, Crosby bought the San Juan ranch off the Tesuque highway a few miles north of Santa Fe.

In 1957, Crosby's opera house opened—the only outdoor opera in America. Designed by John McHugh and Van Dorn Hooker and built for $115,000, the arc-shaped seating arrangement, which seated 480 people, resembled a morning glory horn like those attached to old gramophones. The roof canted upward over stage wings slanting outward past the orchestra pit. These could be left open to reveal the beauty of piñon-covered hills and the New Mexico sky or closed for intimacy. With no fancy boxes, there was not a bad seat in the house—each had a perfect sight line and was acoustically equivalent to the others. At the end of the two-month season, the opera performed to over twelve thousand patrons with 90 percent attendance, taking in $40,700 at the box office.

Tickets sold for $4.80, $3.60, and $2.40. All operas were sung in English to make them easier to stage, act in, and understand. That first season opened with the conventional opera *Madame Butterfly,* which was very well received. As Eleanor Scott said in her booklet *The First Twenty Years of the Santa Fe Opera,*

> Opening night found Crosby wrestling the theater's recalcitrant plumbing, with barely time to exchange monkey wrench for baton. When he stepped onto the podium to summon the first notes of *Madame Butterfly,* the house was sold out. The weather, perfect. There are many who still remember the chorus softly singing as it climbed the moonlit hill and wound its way through piñons to reach the stage, the lights of Los Alamos trembling far on the horizon. It was a moment of magic. Later, when the tenor's final cry of anguish sounded, applause shook the hills, and ten curtain calls followed.

The first year continued with a repertory ranging from *The Barber of Seville* to *The Tower,* a premier of an experimental opera by a young American composer. It also included Mozart's *Cosi Fan Tutte,* Richard Strauss's *Ariadne auf Naxos,* and Stravinsky's *The Rake's Progress.* The Santa Fe Opera had joined the ranks of important festivals and gained the attention of the music world, with *Time* magazine describing it as "one of the handsomest operatic settings in the Western Hemisphere." All this was going on during the era of Elvis Presley and Sputnik, and at the time when the U.S.S.R. sent up the first earth satellite.

Ten years later, Santa Fe's first opera house burned to the ground during the summer opera season. Performances were continued in a high school gymnasium. The twelfth season opened in a new opera house. Built at a cost of $2,200,000, it seated three times as many patrons with many more public amenities, and was known for its famous flared roof, which was open to the sky.

Beginning in 1988 trustees of the opera made plans for yet another building that was completed in 1998; built at a cost of around $18 million and better protects audiences from the elements. In 1996, John Crosby celebrated his seventieth birthday, and the Santa Fe Opera its fortieth. But looking back, in a recent letter designer Van Dorn Hooker, one of the first opera's architects, reminisced about what Santa Fe was like when the first opera was built:

> It was a good time to live in Santa Fe compared to what life there has become. Something like 35,000 people, not too crowded, no traffic problems, not too many tourists, many good friends. But too many architects. We had to do work all over northern New Mexico to make a living.

In autumn, the major celebration was the Fiesta de Santa Fe over Labor Day weekend. Fiesta, which originated in 1712 to commemorate De Vargas's reconquest of Santa Fe from the Indians, played a significant part in the austere lives of early colonists, although some early puritanical Americans saw it as reflecting reckless dissipation and vice that went on night and day.

Then when the United States Army took over the area from Mexico a generation later, Spanish cultural roots were downplayed, and there were more band concerts than fiestas on the Plaza. But over time, Spanish heritage was too important and powerful to be denied. De Vargas was a more significant figure to them than George Washington; and our present Santa Fe Fiesta is now seen as the oldest community celebration in America.

As I wrote in a Chamber of Commerce brochure for tourists, the very word *fiesta* conjures up visions of the event—the color and gaiety of the shifting kaleidoscope of brilliant costumes; the revelry of Medieval Spain reflected in processions and pageants, accompanied by the click of castanets and the jingle of spurs; ripples of laughter during moonlit street dancing in neighborhoods lit up by *farolitos* and *luminarias*.

In the 1950s, Fiesta began on Friday evening with the burning of Zozobra, Old Man Gloom, on the edge of a high hill north of town. The forty-foot dressed-up marionette

(designed in 1924 by Will Shuster, one of the famous Los
Cinco Pintores) flailed his arms and groaned in the flames, as
people torched the giant effigy with fireworks more dramatic
than on the Fourth of July. Following this pagan-like ritual, the
crowd turned back to the Plaza about a mile away, shouting,
"Viva la Fiesta!"

The celebrations continued during the weekend with historical parades of many people in Spanish garb, with small theater productions on the Plaza by special groups, and with
music by sombreroed Spanish mariachis in vests of brilliant
color and metallic decoration. Booths everywhere provided
food and drink, with celebration continuing for many throughout the day and night, ending four event-filled days later in a
gay swirl of street dancing.

Our family at the offices of Kenneth Clark had its own special celebration, known as Hyatt's After Zozobra Bash. I wrote
home about this:

> Saturday I was invited to the Hyatt's After Zozobra
> Bash—a traditional Fiesta party I've always wanted to
> attend. Now that I'm in the architectural family, it's the
> highlight of my Fiesta celebration. The Hyatts live way
> out Canyon Road in a 250-year-old adobe. Along the
> road is a big high adobe wall enclosing a huge patio. The
> walls were topped with lines of *farolitos*—paper bags half
> filled with sand, which hold burning candles that light up
> the bags like big fat ornaments.
>
> We began out in the spacious patio until it started sprin-
> kling. Then we moved inside with a five-piece orchestra
> for dancing, though there wasn't much room inside.
> After the orchestra left at some odd hour, there were two
> gals who could play anything on the piano—all the won-
> derful old songs. Thirty or more of us sang, danced, and
> drank of course.
>
> A featured spot was the Hyatt bathroom! You enter it
> off the flagstone-floored kitchen through a beautifully
> designed wide but low wooden door—designed, I was
> told, to the measurements of the lady of the house. Most

of us had to stoop to go in!

The attraction inside is an antique tin bathtub from the historic Central Hotel, resonation from which made our tipsy voices sound superb! The smallish room was always packed—standing room only, including three in the tub! I stayed on to the end, when about a dozen of us had scrambled eggs and bacon about 4 A.M.

Since the 1950s the traditional Plaza and activities around it have changed considerably. Today, Fiesta de Santa Fe has become a huge, crowded event—no longer such a community celebration reflecting its original historic significance.

Although Indians still sell arts and crafts daily under the portal of the Palace of the Governors, now the largest Indian Market in the world also takes place in Santa Fe in August. At times, six hundred or more booths fill the block under the portal and the surrounding Plaza area. Hotel rooms are reserved a year in advance. Sometimes huge crowds around the booths make it impossible to even see the artwork. Prices are high, and lots of money changes hands, though many pieces are purchased in advance by moneyed patrons.

Throughout the year there are smaller arts and crafts fairs from time to time, which are more relaxed and fun to attend. Some residents feel that the genuine community Plaza event that Fiesta used to be is now the colorful breakfast on the Fourth of July. Along with dancers, bands, singers, and spontaneous activities, locals join tourists in an old-fashioned get-together.

The Plaza park is much the same as in the 1950s, although I heard an interesting story about the center monument that illustrates how times have changed. The monument was placed there to commemorate those who died fighting the Indians. Some years ago a well-intentioned young man took it upon himself to climb the iron rail fence around the monument and chisel out the offensive word *savage*, which appeared on the monument describing the Indians. He apparently did not realize that it was actually the term the Pueblo Indians used historically to refer to the nomadic Navajos who plundered their crops and stole their children.

The Plaza area itself has changed a lot since the l950s. The buildings surrounding it are now mostly expensive boutiques, galleries, and shops containing Indian artifacts designed for the tourist trade. Since Woolworth closed stores nationwide, only one establishment from the l950s still remains—the old Plaza Cafe, run by a local Greek family. It recently celebrated its fiftieth anniversary at that location.

A special friend in our Kenneth Clark family was structural engineer Pat Wood, who had a particular interest in eccentric characters around Santa Fe. He was especially fascinated with one familiar to all of us—Tommy Macaione, an artist known for his sunflowers. Pat sent me the following newspaper clipping from Hollis Walker's column in the *New Mexican:*

> Pat Wood sent over some personal remembrances of the late painter and town character Tommy Macaione this week, prompted by Wednesday's fund raiser for the sculpture of Tommy to be created by Mac Vaughan. Wood, who has lived in Santa Fe since 1948, recalled driving east on Armenta Road one summer day many years ago when he spotted Tommy painting sunflowers as the sun began to set. I pulled the old '55 Chevy wagon off the road to the right as quietly as I could, and turned off the motor. He glanced at me and said: "I've got to hurry! The sun's about to set!" Wood offered to give Tommy a ride when he was done, but the frantic painter said he had a ride. About five minutes later a cab pulled up. The driver got out, opened the trunk, helped Tommy put his easel, palette and paints into the trunk, carefully placed the painting on the back seat, opened the passenger side door in front, held it as if for royalty, and slowly closed it after Tommy got in. As they were driving away, Tommy rolled his window down and shouted to me, "I owe my soul to the Yellow Cab Company!"

In his letter to me, Pat shared his own eulogy for Tommy

Macaione:

> The last time I saw Tommy was at his eightieth birthday
> party at the Fine Arts Museum downtown. I didn't stay
> long, but I'm glad I went. The pervading feeling was love
> and gaiety. Tommy was having a ball, standing on a table
> and leading the caroling in his Santa Claus suit. The icing
> on the cake had to have been done by Tommy with his
> smallest pallet knife. It was our mountains, covered with
> green pine trees and golden aspens in the Macione style.
> I'm grateful to have had the chance to have eaten a little
> piece of a Tommy painting. Good-bye Tommy! You've
> been our greatest character ever since painter Alfred
> Morang died.

I also remembered Tommy as a bushy-haired, bearded exu-
berant personality, a bit of an exhibitionist in a nice sort of way.
I heard that he often gave paintings to people who bought him
groceries, since he was always poor. He usually smelled of dogs
because he picked up strays and kept so many of them (some
said as many as twenty) until he was forced to give them up.
Despite his eccentricities, he was a much-loved character; and
a sculpture of Tommy at his easel, made by a fellow artist, now
stands in Hillside Park.

Pat also reminisced about another Santa Fe character who
we were accustomed to seeing riding around town on a little
red Italian Vespa motor scooter, with his huge-brimmed flat-
topped Bee Bee Dunn hat and his vicuna coat blowing wildly
out behind. Pat said:

> I believe that Bee Bee was the personal secretary of
> Senator Bronson Cutting. He rented out a rather large
> adobe house off of what is now Paseo de Peralta; and one
> day a car ran off the road and smacked into the house. It
> totally demolished the front of the car, but hardly dented
> the house. Bee Bee explained to the *New Mexican* news-
> paper that the reason the house had so little damage was
> that the adobe block wall was clad in a layer of steel. He

was referring, of course, to the chicken wire placed over the adobe to help the stucco adhere to the wall. This chicken wire is so thin that it wouldn't even stop a small chicken. Oh well, Bee Bee freely used his, he felt, God-given right to exaggerate.

During the day he practically lived in the lobby of the La Fonda Hotel. They still have his light brown vicuna coat stuffed in a plexiglass box about one foot square and three feet tall, in the lobby of the La Fonda. My thought when I saw it was: Couldn't they at least have hung it up?

In regard to special artists, I recall a collection of Foster Hyatt's blowgun renderings of picturesque adobe village churches of the area, which he first sent out to friends as Christmas cards over the years. They now decorate a long wall in the current New Mexico Capitol, built in the early 1950s.

Some of my architect friends worked on the design of the present Territorial-style capitol building between Galisteo and Don Gaspar not far from the Plaza across the Alameda. The flags of four nations have flown over that oldest capitol of our country—Spain, Mexico, the Confederacy, and the United States. The original building, constructed in 1892, was a towering Victorian structure of stone surrounded by a low stone wall in a treeless field. This was replaced in 1900 by a building with two wings and a central dome, which was New Mexico's capitol until the present building was built in the 1950s while I was there.

As a single person, my friends connected with Kenneth Clark's offices offered me the family I didn't have, I was greatly enriched by this family and my ever-widening circle of creative friends.

CHAPTER 8

CANYON ADVENTURES and the CARSWELLS' SHED

Another memorable part of my life in Santa Fe that began while I was with the Kenneth Clark family was my association with the Rock Club. In the spring of 1955, David, one of our draftsmen, stopped by my desk and said, "Vi, the Rock Club is going on a trip Sunday. Would you like to come along?" Although I have not said yes to a man in marriage, I have often made spontaneous decisions which have had enormous consequences. I said yes to David that morning; and after that first trip I was hooked as a rockhound, not only because New Mexico is a treasure trove of great natural mineral locations, but because I realized rockhounds were my kind of people.

The Rock Club was fortunate to have Walt and Alma Wright as professionals. Walt had been a civil engineer in the East who had succumbed to his first love of rocks and minerals. The Wrights had come to Santa Fe and opened a rock shop on lower San Francisco Street. It was wonderful for beginners like me to have the Wrights along on trips that took us to fascinating spots in the mountains I would otherwise never have seen.

Most members of the club knew a lot about rocks and minerals. However, I knew nothing—so hesitated to ask foolish questions. Although I did go to the library, the books I found on the subject seemed either too elementary or too advanced for me; and I kept saying, "Someone ought to write a book for the mature amateur who doesn't have a scientific background."

Through the Rock Club I met Dr. Dan Elliot, a millionaire bachelor and a professor of mineralogy at an eastern college. During World War II our government had commissioned him to scout for deposits of strategic minerals across the country.

119

He had found an interesting beryllium deposit in northern
New Mexico; and when the government was not interested, he
bought the land and hired some Spanish men to work it. He
would come out summers to see how his mine was doing, and
joined us on some of our jaunts. Dr. Dan took us on a trip to
the Taos area, where we found unbelievable specimens of gar-
net crystals and staurolite in mica schist. Staurolites are exciting to look for, especially for beginners, since their fat opaque
brown prism crystals penetrate each other to make perfect
right-angle crosses.

Our Rock Club went on several exciting trips to hidden
mines or canyons in the surrounding mountains. On one
unforgettable trip, two carloads of us decided to get accommodations and stay over to spend the next day searching for a
cave supposedly lined with selenite crystals.

We started off on a one-way road for several miles, finally
stopping as we came to a tiny village, where teachers and students walked out of the small schoolhouse when they heard us,
because they seldom saw anyone from outside their community. At another location we had to stop while David tossed rocks
off the road. Further on, the narrow road led us into a box
canyon with flat steps our station wagon could not climb. We
had to stop, but wondered whether the road might have been
made to lead to the particular canyon we were looking for.

Then someone recalled a place we had passed where tire
tracks had taken off from the road. We headed back and followed the tracks, which led us to the edge of a wide canyon.
At the rim the driver of one of the cars turned back to get
home by the long way we'd come.

We then followed a precarious road down into the canyon,
and on the other side were astonished to meet a long-bearded
man who lived in a tiny shack beside a small garden. When we
asked about how to get out of there, he said, pointing, "A year
ago a man kept going along the side of that mountain over
there, and he didn't come back. But he was driving a jeep."
Although we told him our goal, he said he'd never heard of

such a cave. However, our spirit of adventure held out, even though we weren't sure we were in the right area. Consequently, we spent till late afternoon traversing the back side of this mountain, stopping several times when we came to a steep grade while we calculated whether the station wagon would get hung up trying to switch directions.

We did not find the cave. And as we came to the end of the range and the road flattened out across fields toward the highway, we were stopped by two men prospecting along a creek bed. They said they could not believe their eyes when seeing a car come out of that valley. As we finally connected with a paved double-lane highway heading north to Santa Fe, we had a feeling of coming home from a foreign land. Such experiences were what made rockhounding in New Mexico so memorable.

Hoping to share my excitement about such adventures with others, I sent an article entitled "Tracking Down Treasure" to *New Mexico Suntrails,* which had published my article about the trail ride. Weeks went by before I got a letter from the editor, saying, "I have two things to tell you. First of all, I plan to use your article; and second, I mentioned it to Mr. E. B. Mann, director of the University of New Mexico Press, who told me he was looking for someone to write a book on minerals, and wondered whether Miss K. would be interested." In my reply I said, "I know nothing about minerals," but he answered, "Why not write Mr. Mann anyway."

I did write Mr. Mann that I didn't have the background to do what he had in mind, but shared my feeling that books on the subject in the library were either too simple or far too complex and that he should look for someone to publish a book for rockhounds like me who didn't have a scientific background. His reply: "It sounds interesting. I can't make you any promises; but why don't you go ahead."

This may have been the beginning of my writing career; for in my excitement I envisioned a book entitled *Minerals from Mountains to Molecules,* with the thought that minerals truly run the gamut of the sciences. To know where to find a mineral specimen, you have to know in which rock you might find it, along with some physical geology on how mountains are formed and worn down. This would put you in touch with historical geology and the theories of how the earth originated. Then, when you had a mineral specimen, you would need to know its physical properties, its chemical composition, and its crystallography, which would bring you to basic atomic theories.

For the next three years, I happily researched and wrote, until I met Tim Sanders, who changed my interests. Despite the fact that this manuscript was never published, I still treasure my rockhounding days in New Mexico in ways difficult to express except in poetry. In the closing lines of a poem entitled "Perspectives," I said:

> The grains of sand, life-giving earth,
> from which emerges endless kinds of growth—
> the stones and rocks, each with a history of its own,
> so much wonder at—so much unknown.

Another significant aspect of life at this time was my friendship with two weavers who were to open a famous Santa Fe restaurant—Polly and Thornton Carswell.

I'd first met the Carswells in my days at the Chamber of Commerce—when I had taken Jim Madison to the Ski Basin during Aspen Week. In returning down the mountain to Santa Fe, we passed the old Hyde Park Lodge, which had been closed, and gasped at an unbelievable sign on a tree that said "Snack Bar." I stopped, drove in to investigate, and parked the car.

Just inside the door on a deck were five high stools at a counter. We climbed up and ordered sandwiches and drinks from a genial man in his forties. A pleasingly plump, round-faced woman, who was the picture of good health, brought our order, setting it out with a sunny smile. I said, "I never expected to find a snack bar up here. How did it happen?" We heard the story as we ate our sandwiches.

Polly and Thornton Carswell were both weavers from Carmel, California, who had come to Santa Fe and were overtaken with that need to stay—that need felt by so many creative people. On a drive up the mountain, they had stopped at the lodge and talked with Mr. Steele, the caretaker. Apparently, without official inquiry, he had told them they could live there. Polly, who I discovered later was a fantastic cook, asked me that day, "Just how do you cook beans here?" She was to learn that at an altitude of around 8,000 feet, water boils at a much lower temperature, and it takes quite a bit longer to cook or bake things. This is how I met Polly and Thornton Carswell, who became lifelong friends. Little did I realize then that Jim Madison and I were talking to the couple who were to become historic Santa Feans, feeding practically every tourist who came to Santa Fe at their well-known restaurant The Shed.

I visited the Carswells while they were living at Hyde Park and loved driving up through the tall pines. They hadn't moved many belongings from California, so their furnishings were sparse and primitive in the spacious log lodge; but it was acceptable for summer living.

One Saturday night Jack and I were invited to the lodge for dinner. Polly had called to tell us, "There's an interesting man camping at the park with a young Mexican. We think he's pretty special, and we'd like you to meet him."

On the way up the hill, it started to rain and continued all evening. The dim glow of lamplight and the steady drip, drip from roof leaks into pails and pans on the floor made a perfect setting for the tall Canadian poet. Bob Sheward read poetry from his recent book *Tuna Eaters,* printed in Mexico. When he couldn't pay the border tax after the printing, he had made a deal to enter the United States by tearing off the covers. Later, he sent me a copy inscribed, "To Vi, in memory of the night we dodged raindrops and played canasta. June 6, 1955. Bob Sheward."

That night it did not take much begging for Bob to keep reading. He moved beneath a lamp on a high shelf. And with lamplight burnishing his coppery blonde hair, he began with the first verse of "Aquamarine or Jade":

> The gulf is a golden dream again
> That laughs in a reckless way,
> Calling as only the sea can call,
> Calling me back to the dreams of man,
> Calling me back to the carefree day
> When I laughed and lost and went away,
> And the light went out and the sky turned gray,
> And nobody cared at all.

That night Bob told us that he had to go back to Mexico to pick up a ten-year-old boy with no nose he had found hiding in an old building daytimes to avoid being teased. Evidently a chemical in some nose drops his mother had used had eaten the boy's nose. Bob planned to take the boy to Phoenix, where a surgeon he knew could arrange for restoration surgery. Later, I got a letter from Bob saying that the surgery had taken place, and that the boy was ecstatic about the outcome and had screamed, "My nose! I have a nose!"

Around this time Polly and Thornton decided they had to live in the City Different and made arrangements to move their belongings from California. The next time I was their guest was at their little house on Rodriguiz Street—a small adobe they transformed into a warm home with draperies from Polly's loom and rugs from Thornton's. Thornton worked to support the family as a linotype operator at the newspaper, but often spent time weaving Saturdays and Sundays.

I loved the two Carswell boys, who were also artists. Courtney often brought me crayon sketches, which were the impetus for my file of children's art I have collected over the years, treasuring its exciting imagination and spontaneity. Courtney had a great imagination for his age. One evening when the Carswells came over for dinner he brought me a crayon drawing of high mountains with a small dark rectangle way up on the side of one peak near the top. Intrigued, I asked, "What's that Courtney?" "Oh, Vi, that's a telephone booth. I thought it would come in handy if somebody climbed the peak and got in trouble."

Although Thornton and Polly were accomplished craftspeople who sold their weavings, one day in wandering around town they were struck by the idea that Santa Fe needed another restaurant. On that day they stopped to chat with Walt and Alma Wright at their rock shop on San Francisco Street a few blocks from the Plaza. Then they decided to investigate West San Francisco Street, which was a kind of slum area in the 1950s, and had apparently been the red light district of Santa Fe in the early days. They turned on the first street off to the right—a narrow lane called Burro Alley. Soon on the right they saw a narrow path leading to a small plaza, where there was a long open lean-to with a corrugated metal roof; and suddenly they envisioned this as a possible location for a restaurant

In a matter of weeks, this lean-to was to become the birthplace of the best-loved Santa Fe restaurant, known to every tourist for years to come. Establishing the restaurant from the open lean-to involved installing a kitchen and dining area, plastering, painting, decorating, and laying flagstone for an outdoor dining area. I gladly became involved in the project as I painted the ladies room a lovely lemon yellow. When it was finished, they called the restaurant The Shed—a name selected by Polly.

The attractive menus, which guests were encouraged to take as souvenirs, were brown with a deeper brown sketch of the patio and lean-to with burros and their packs to illustrate the Burro Alley story on the front cover, which said:

In the old days, Burro Alley was a popular spot with the wood merchants. These men sold their wood by the burro-load, and strings of piñon-laden burros were a common sight in the ancient city. After the wood was sold, the burros were turned into the corral (which is now the patio) with the owners' coats over their heads. This discouraged the burros from straying and helped the owner identify his burro when he returned from the Cantina under a load of "Mula Blanc."

Inside, the tables were set with southwestern pottery and blue and brown Mexican glassware. On the menu, hamburgers started at $.50 and went to $1.00, with cheese (American or Swiss). Boston beans with green salad was $1.00, coffee or tea $.10 (iced, $.15), pies (including my favorite, pecan) were $.20. Although for dinner you could always order a steak or chops, Polly had a specialty each day of the week for $2.00. Monday was veal scallopini with egg noodles, fresh or frozen vegetables, tossed green salad, French bread, dessert, and tea or coffee. Tuesday was lamb with prunes, Swedish style. Wednesday was beef stroganoff with cracked wheat, Thursday was chicken cacciatore with polenta, and Friday was shrimp curry with saffron rice and condiments.

In 1960, the original Shed was torn down to make way for a new office building; and The Shed restaurant moved to Prince Plaza with a lovely courtyard, next door to Sena Plaza. After Polly's death, the restaurant was run by Thornton and Courtney until Thornton's death in 1986. The restaurant's ad says, "Serving Santa Fe Since 1955. For 40 Years the Place Where Locals Go for a Taste of New Mexico."

During this time Polly Carswell, Jack, and other friends encouraged me to get involved with some cultural activities and to travel around the Southwest. One spring, I hit the doldrums. Jack was down for dinner, and during conversation I shared a feeling, "If I were to die tomorrow, no one would really care." Jack scolded me for having such a thought. "Hey, gal, you know that's ridiculous. You've got to do something about such wild feelings." At one point I said, "Well, at home when I felt like this, I could go bang on the piano; but I don't have one here."

Jack was a man of action, and said, "Surely if you really want a piano you could rent one." He was right; and the next day, when I happened to mention this conversation to my landlady, Wilma said, "The Martins next door have one they never use. I'll bet they'd rent it." So, within two days I had my piano; and though I didn't use it much, it helped.

Jack kept encouraging me to get involved with more local activities; and one day I heard of a ceramics class. When I mentioned it to Polly, she got excited and said, "Oh yes, Vi, I've heard that Bud Gilbertson's doing it. He's got quite a reputation—studied in Korea. Let's do it!" So we signed up. Polly and I had been spending a lot of time together. We found we had both been German Lutherans as children but had questioned some of the theology. Because we felt it would be good to belong to a church, we picked out and attended a Lutheran congregation but were discouraged by the same old reward-and-punishment theology and gave up on the quest.

Unfortunately, the day before the ceramics class was to begin Polly called to cancel, saying, "Vi, we just can't afford the $25.00. I thought about canceling, too, but didn't wish to face friends with an excuse I didn't have. So I enrolled in the class, which turned out to be another of my favorite Santa Fe experiences.

Bud Gilbertson's studio was in a sprawling adobe way out on the outskirts of Santa Fe. I was eager to see the inside, for vintage adobes are unique—no two are alike. This adobe had walls of different heights in odd places, with adobe fireplaces built with a stovepipe in corners covered with clay to the ceiling.

That first class meeting was in the spacious living room filled with lots of people, many of them focused on a woman seated in the center speaking. I was struck by her attractive animated face beneath an unusual hairdo for Santa Fe, and joined in listening to her conversation, which was pitched in the kind of voice that suggested self-centered high society to this middle-class Midwesterner. It turned me off; and I moved to a seat in a far corner to listen judgmentally as the woman related how she had come to Santa Fe that summer to "do something in the third dimension," meaning taking this class and another in sculpting.

This character, with whom I later became friends, turned out to be Carolin Witherspoon, a wealthy divorcée who had worked in theater therapy in veterans hospitals and had come to Santa Fe because of its reputation in the art world. We both joined the class; and I thought again of what I'd learned from Jack—that one should try a bit of everything—that in a pottery or say a silver class, if nothing else, one could gain appreciation for what is involved in producing a good pot or piece of silver.

Had pottery been one of my strengths, I no doubt would have thrived under Bud Gilbertson. He was an excellent instructor, admired in Santa Fe and across the country. In the July 20, 1953, issue of *Time* magazine, he was featured in the art section with his picture and an article entitled "Classics in Clay," part of which said:

> One notable weakness of most contemporary art has been the decline in artistic craftsmanship. Among the exceptions to the rule is a lanky Santa Fe potter named Warren Gilbertson, 42, who combines the artist's soaring imagination with the craftsman's practical knowledge of his tools. Last week he was demonstrating the fact anew with a series of glowing vases, cups and bowls which looked extraordinarily like China's classic Sung Dynasty Chien-yao ware (better known by its Japanese name: Temmoku). The secret of making it has been lost for about 750 years. Experimenting over the past few months with a variety of natural clays and fusing materials, Gilbertson finally managed to produce a glaze almost indistinguishable from the Temmoku. Says he of his formulas: "It's my secret now."

Carolin loved cats and made pottery decorated with cat motifs. When Gilbertson, whom we called Gil, criticized this work and suggested more abstract lines, she flared up. Speaking of two women in the class, who'd joined late and whom I felt because of their lack of creativity Gil had let do anything they wished, Carolin said, "He'll let those girls get by making those goddamned little mushrooms, and then picks on me!"

When Carolin invited me to dinner several times after class,

I kept politely refusing, finding excuses. But one evening three of us stayed after class to talk with Gil, and about eleven we organized an expedition to find some food. With most restaurants closed, we ended up at a spot way out on Cerrillos Road; and because Carolin lived in my part of town, I took her home. As we stopped in front of her apartment just off Camino del Monte Sol, she said, "Well now, Vi, you'll know where I live the next time I ask you to dinner. How about a nightcap?"

Since I have a way of saying yes in serendipitous situations, I ended up drinking I forget how many Southern Comfort and Creme de Cocoa southern belles with Carolin, and this evening turned out to be the beginning of a lifelong friendship. That night we talked till two in the morning; and though we were opposites in many ways, we found there were many interests we had in common, which we were to explore during the next six months.

In addition to her uppity way of speaking, Carolin named things, such as her toothbrush and her large Chrysler coupe, which was Puddy Cat. Ordinarily I would have written off a person with such habits; but Carolin was somehow charmingly different. As a friend she was most understanding.

Over the long Fourth of July weekend, we took off in Puddy Cat to explore the northwestern part of New Mexico. At Chaco Canyon we wandered around the fabulous ruins— the ancient apartment houses of another time and race. After crossing the Continental Divide six times that day, we ended up for the night at sprawling vintage El Rancho—one of the best places to stay in Gallup in those days when the town was only a line of stores, restaurants, and gas stations on U. S. Route 66. The next morning we were off to Canyon de Chelly, smiling at the invitation of the black doorman as he helped load our car to, "Come back." We didn't ever expect to.

It took hours to cover the hundred miles or more to Canyon de Chelly on washboard roads with lots of curves and potholes. But our impatience disappeared as we approached the canyon rim. We got out of the car and stood there in silent awe! The famed ruins of storied dwellings carved in a niche toward the bottom of a sheer vertical wall were tiny specks from the top.

Carolin said, "Vi, I know you're going to want to go down into the canyon to get some pictures. I've brought a book to read. I'll wait up here." So off I went to try to somehow capture on film that unique setting and to wonder about a home in a tiny niche way up on that sheer pink-tan cliff. Why had the Indians picked that spot, and why had they left? I was intrigued with many questions about an ancient past that made the history of the Southwest so fascinating.

After I climbed back up and shared my discoveries and wonder with Carolin, we drove along the canyon rim to Spider Rock, a tall free-standing monolith about halfway out in a kind of crossroads of the canyon. Something firm on top must have saved it from historic elements that had carved out the rest of the canyon. There I took more pictures, as Carolin dragged the picnic stuff to the edge of the cliff for a late bite as we drank in the view. While we were eating, I looked back up the canyon. Startled, I yelled out, "Carolin—look, look! That's a sheet of rain moving in on us." It actually was a moving vertical curtain. We were mesmerized into watching, becoming enveloped in a cloudburst as the curtain reached us and we were inside.

After moments which seemed hours, we made it back to the car and just sat there for a moment, wondering what to do as we looked at the one-lane road winding up a steep hill. If this trail were caliche, we were in for it. And so we were! Caliche is a kind of earth that sticks to everything when wet. In backing the car around to start up the long hill, we found the surface of the road like thick caramel icing on a cake. Puddy Cat's tires kept picking up more and more mud till we could hardly move. When I got out, the same thing happened to me. Each time I'd pick up a foot, it would be a bigger glob of oozy mud, until I felt I had on a pair of snowshoes.

I pulled up cactus from the muddy goo, put it beneath the wheels, and we'd move ahead only to slide back again. Finally, little by little, we reached the hard left curve at the top of the hill, where Puddy Cat slid in the ditch. Then, as Carolin would give the car gas and spin the wheels, we'd make a kind of bird pattern as we'd settle back in the ditch. We looked at the free-form pattern we'd made and started laughing, for we knew Gil would have approved.

After many attempts, we finally crested the top of the hill and stopped at Stinkey Mac's Snack Shack to ask what he thought of trying to get back to Gallup. He thought we could make it if we took it easy, so we were off. That hundred miles was a long nightmare. With washouts in the road, we'd have to find our way around with old Puddy Cat swishing her tail back and forth in the slippery goo. At one point we were entirely blinded as a Navajo Patrol passed us, covering our windshield in mud so we couldn't see the road. To see again, we had to find a puddle of some unmuddy water to clear our view. It was after midnight as we once again drove up to El Rancho, where the same black doorman, with a big understanding grin, listened to our story.

One day of our trip was left. At dawn we started off to Mesa Verde in southwestern Colorado. As we neared the ruins, I drove a winding uphill road twenty miles through rain and dense fog. Even at the top it was disappointing not to be able to see the famous ruins; so I said, "Let's go have lunch. I have a feeling the weather will clear." Later, we smiled at the prediction as we emerged from the restaurant to see a blue sky piled high with fluffy white cumulus clouds.

We toured the amazing historic Mesa Verde cliff dwelling ruins, so beautifully designed and tucked away under the overhanging cliffs of prairie land. Once again I wondered about the Anasazi, the Ancient Ones, who apparently were ancestors of our New Mexico Tewas. Why had they built the apartment-like dwellings at that site, and why had they abandoned them?

On the way out, we shuddered as we saw the road we'd come up in the fog, and how there was a sheer drop-off along a razor-sharp cliff. It was a long drive back to Santa Fe, but under bright starry skies and a full moon. Only those who have lived in the Southwest know such nights, where stars are so bright and close you feel you can reach up and pick a whole handful.

In August, Carolin and I returned to Gallup for the Intertribal Indian Ceremonial. I wrote home about it:

We left at six in the morning for the 200-mile drive to Gallup. Carolin had out-of-town guests, so we took two cars, and I drove with her friend Bill. Gallup is a town of around nine thousand; but the papers said that some twenty-five thousand outsiders came for the ceremonial. The place was jam-packed—not only with curious tourists but with Indians from as far as South Dakota and Oklahoma. Bill had an old friend there whose name I thought sounded familiar. It turned out to be my friend Lee Langan, who was secretary of the Gallup Chamber of Commerce and was manager of the Indian Ceremonial.

We found the place we were to stay. After freshening up we were invited to the Langans for a drink and luncheon. Kitty Langan came out to meet us and said, "Perhaps I'd better warn you. We have twenty-six people staying with us. I don't know quite where, but they'll be in and out. The phone rings every five minutes. We have everything from grownups to ten year olds, plus two nuns!" She was right. It was like a ten-ring circus.

At one point a boy came in putting down a white cloth sack. We thought nothing of it till there was a rattling sound and Kitty yelled, "Bill, what's in that sack?" Nonchalantly Bill said, "Oh that's just a rattlesnake I picked up this morning." After we calmed down following that little episode, we laughed and agreed it truly was much like "You Can't Take It With You," and wondered whether there was someone in the basement making fireworks!

Following drinks and dinner at the Country Club that evening, we went to the opening performance, to which Lee brought tickets for great seats we wouldn't have gotten ourselves. We were among the Indians and more entranced in watching them than some of the program. We loved the colorful costumes reflected in the light and shadows of four immense piñon fires. After checking out some of the exhibits of blankets, silver, paintings, and stuff, we ended up at a party at the Langans till early morning.

Sunday we had breakfast at El Rancho, which was all spiffed up on account of that's where Eisenhower was to stay. Again, Lew had gotten us tickets with all the celebrities. We sat near Ike, so we could watch him; and I thought again of what a warm human being he is—of being a dinner guest with him in Berlin.

We were sitting on a sofa listening to a musical before dinner. He'd not been too interested with a singer; but when a little guitarist General Lucius Clay had brought in did her number, Ike asked whether she could play the "Beer-Barrel Polka." As she did, he sat there on the sofa next to me grinning, slapping his leg with, "Boy, that's my regiment's old marching song!"

I saw that very part of him there in Gallup. He quietly watched the Indian dancers and some horse races, but got a big kick out of a little ten year old who won a special race. They used cowhides which had been wet and then dried over a fence and so were like folded in half. These were tied with a long rope to a horse and rider. Then an Indian sits between the folds and gets dragged, having to go around a marker and back. Only one of them made it—that little ten year old; and Ike loved it! There was bulldogging and steer roping, even watermelon races.

We left after the show and at about seven started for home, taking a turnoff to Acoma—the Sky City. It's an Indian pueblo built atop a huge free-standing mesa with sheer walls which you have to climb by a path with footholds. Saw it all by late sunset and almost darkness— the huge wonderful church by flashlight. After dinner in Albuquerque and coffee again in Santa Fe, I got to bed at 2:30. And this coming week will be busy getting ready for Edith to arrive on Friday.

Edith was a hometown friend from Minnesota. It's really to her I owed being in Santa Fe. I mentioned the letter she had written me when I was in Europe during World War II about Santa Fe being like the Garmisch I loved in Bavaria. So I wanted to share as much of my beloved pink and blue country with Edith as I could. Over the Labor Day weekend we drove south to White Sands Proving Grounds and Carlsbad Caverns.

Edith was fascinated when I told her that White Sands was not made of sand but was the product of wind, sun, and rain—that dunes are born of water seeping through slopes of surrounding mountains, eating away gypsum deposits, which later the sun dries into gypsum crystals. So White Sands consisted of trillions of gypsum crystals that had been moved over the years by the wind to cover more than two hundred and seventy square miles.

Before we had left, Carolin had said, "I'll take care of Jack for you, Vi." Upon our return, I discovered the two had had a high old time, even seeing a flying saucer cross the sky on their way back from dinner one night. At least that was their story! UFOs had been in the news in New Mexico in 1947 when it was rumored that one had crashed at Roswell. Recently, I read an article in the May 31, 1997, issue of *U.S. News & World Report* entitled "Roswell Makes Commercial Contact." It reported that, as with the Rosenberg story, there were questions as to whether or not the government had covered up the truth about a UFO crash in Roswell. Whatever the truth, the incident has recently made the town a UFO center attracting thousands of tourists.

Early that winter an unfortunate event prompted Carolin and I to take another harrowing trip—this time to Colorado. Jack's doctor discovered a spot on his lung, and he was sent to a special hospital in Denver. Carolin offered to join me on a trip to see him. The day before we were to leave we'd had an unusual snowstorm; and when we called about the roads, we were told that they were "clear in spots!" Nevertheless, we decided to go; and in addition to icy roads, we had to dodge large birds that had come to feast on other wildlife killed on the warm road. At one point, when we disturbed a large crow, it skidded up over the hood and windshield as Carolin cried out, "Look at that crazy bird backing into us!"

We had a good visit with Jack; and his long stay in Denver proved just the kind of break I needed to come to terms with our relationship. Jack was a Catholic when he came to Los Alamos, and we had talked about his questioning some of his religious beliefs. However, a young priest in Denver had convinced him that his scientific beliefs were not at odds with his religious beliefs and not to be concerned. When he told me that, we never again mentioned religion.

Jack and I had had wonderful times together that had been more than a mere friendship, even though we had never been intimate. He was a fun companion and teacher, but I could not envision him as a husband. At the same time, with the long Denver days in bed, and time spent with the young Catholic priest, physicist Jack realized that what he'd always wanted to be was a physician. As a result, he made future plans to leave Los Alamos and go to medical school in Texas, where he later married a Catholic woman.

I sometimes reflect on our different paths in light of the fact that I've never married. I often tell the story that when I went to the European Theater with the American Red Cross in Europe during World War II, I felt that any man who'd been raised correctly did not proposition women. But it didn't take long to find this an illusion and be able to categorize the lines I'd hear over and over again. At the time, I turned down serious proposals, feeling the war atmosphere was too artificial in which to make a lifetime decision.

During the 1956 Christmas holidays, I was reconnected with my World War II days. Indiana friends who were in the floral business wrote that they had a ticket for me to join them for the Rose Bowl game in Pasadena if I could come. I got time off from work and over the holidays stayed with Carolin, who had moved to California. She threw a cocktail party for some of her Hollywood friends and invited Bob and Ev Houser. Bob had been one of my close World War II friends with whom I'd kept in touch, who had married Ev and lived in a Los Angeles suburb. I then spent an overnight with the Housers before returning to Santa Fe.

On the trip home, I thought of Bob and of Jack. Bob had been more than a friend during two whole years in Europe, and had continued our relationship after returning to the States; but there was an age difference. I often say today that I have had more significant relationships with men than most married women, and have ended up with unusual male friendships which have continued over the years, even after the men married other women.

I've since discussed these relationships with a clergy friend, who explained his concept of intimacy, answering some of my questions. He suggested that my friendships with men had involved an adult commitment to an open and honest relationship with no hiding behind all kinds of disguises. He felt it could happen only between those who were sure enough of themselves to be open to a state of vulnerability by sharing their innermost desires and needs, their deepest fears and wildest dreams, without being afraid of losing control or being dominated. From that time on, I began to see these relationships as a kind of honest maturity that had nothing to do with age, a perspective that helped me better understand the ending of my relationship with Jack. It had been a good relationship, but one which was more like that between father and daughter, with me often accepting his advice in situations.

Jack and I did not keep in touch after his Catholic marriage some years later. That was half a century ago, when staying single was a questionable state in the eyes of society, before the freedom regarding marital status was to come with the beginning of the women's movement.

CHAPTER 9

- -

GEORGIA O'KEEFFE'S ABIQUIU and the UNITARIANS

Just as I had been close to Audrey and Al in my early Santa Fe days, during the time I worked in Kenneth Clark's office I was adopted into the Walker family. Louie had been a draftsman at our business before he started an architectural consulting office with Nicki as his partner. They were always together.

The road leading to the Walkers' sprawling adobe home, in an arroyo of an old historic part of Santa Fe, took off downhill at an angle from Camino Santander. They'd purchased two adobe shacks as the nucleus of what became one of the most unique homes in Santa Fe. A spacious entry on the first level, where the kitchen and bedroom were located, led to a wide-open arched stairway down into a spacious living room. Then more steps descended through an interesting partially-enclosed patio to the office and drafting room building. Most of the rooms had flagstone floors; and I felt a part of the overall project, volunteering to experiment on hands and knees in finding the right surfacing for the flagstone floors.

The Walkers and I spent many an evening in the office building talking and painting. Louie and Nicki both painted and got me interested in watercolor, which I came to love. It was something I'd never thought of doing; but having all the materials to work with and two instructors to eagerly watch, I experienced a high that comes after creating an expression all one's own; and I still experience the feeling when looking at a framed painting of New Mexico mountainsides at aspen time.

If we were lucky and Louie was flush when the liquor store manager called to say, "We just got in our ration of Jack Daniels," we would sip that good sour-mash whiskey to mellow an evening. And if we talked until late, I would sleep in the roofed part of the unusual connecting patio. There, through a broad window from the high banco, I could view the outside starry sky or look across the patio to exotic flowering plants.

I thought of the Walkers as pioneers when years later I read an article about architect-designer Alexander Girard. He had uprooted his family from a fashionable suburban home in Grosse Point, Michigan, and resettled them in a spreading primitive adobe in Santa Fe, which he proceeded to transform into one of the most trendsetting homes in America. Like Louie Walker, Girard seemed entranced with the marvelous possibilities for experimentation with adobe, and was known for his conversation pit—a large, sunken circular pew-like seating arrangement around a fireplace.

Louie and Nicki had two children. Lou II was eight, and his sister Pill Pot was five. The Walkers had a jeep to use in the area for their jobs or local business; but when we took off on long trips, Old Vintage was the choice—an ancient Oldsmobile with a powerful engine inside a large black superstructure on four big high tires. Even though it seemed out of place on New Mexico roads, it took us on fabulous trips like the one along the Royal Gorge in Colorado.

We left on that trip late one Friday afternoon, heading north toward the Colorado border. Before long it started raining and poured all the way to our overnight destination—the Colorado Great Sand Dunes, which I hadn't known were there. We pulled off the highway and followed a road between some rather high dunes to a flat spot under a single big tree. The kids were sleepy, and all of us were tired, hungry, and damp as we got out in the rain. Louie worked miracles in somehow getting a fire going and into a big enough blaze for Nicki to melt fat in an iron kettle and fry pork chops, which were manna from heaven. Then we put up a tent for the night.

By morning the sky had cleared; and after playing around on wind-dried dunes with Lou II and Pill Pot, we took off, reaching the Royal Gorge by late afternoon. We left the car and walked to the edge. As we looked across and down to the bottom of that wide-open space, it was breathtaking.

We celebrated our arrival in style, with Jack Daniels complementing crackers and smoked oysters, all served on a red and white checked cloth spread on a broad flat stone at the edge of the gorge. As we relaxed in the expansive glory that stretched out before us, we could understand how it got its name.

I was pleased to spend Christmas of 1958 with the Walker family. That year I was concerned about the nuclear threat of contamination, and frequently remarked to friends that children grow up with fallout in their milk. I expressed some of these disturbing Cold War feelings in the greetings I sent to friends across the country and even to England and Germany:

You know I always have to preach, so no doubt you will be
     prepared,
By what I have to say this year you'll see that I am truly
     scared.
I think that we should really be a little apprehensive; and
     in our resolutions, plan a personal offensive.

To give you all some motivation, I'd like to make an
     observation.
When I came back from overseas, I'd spent four years with
     foreigners,
And had three feelings as I put my feet back on this shore
     of ours.

The first—we're snobs, we know it all! In fact, we think
     we're paragons,
No one can tell us anything, just cause we are Americans.

The second, was a case in point. Our culture—what a thin
     veneer,
We blithely think we dig the best; but how transparent is
     our boast!

The third thing, even way back then, we looked askance
    as anyone
Who read a liberal magazine with connotations that can mean.

Our kids have always had the best of schools and clothes
    and food and all
That bucks can buy we always thought; but really, now,
    what has it bought?

We've set examples by the score for all the world to
    wonder at—
Free thought, free speech, equality, McCarthy, Little Rock,
    and more!

Might still be dreaming, flying blind, had Sputnik not crept
    up behind
And pricked our great big gas balloon by sending up a
    brand new moon!
We owe those Russian chaps our thanks for bringing us
    back down to earth.

I went on and on but ended with some special feelings that
started bothering me about that time. I was beginning to wonder how long I should stay in Santa Fe.

And as for me, I go along in pleasant ruts I've been too long,
Just waiting for some motivation to change the place or
    occupation.
But till that comes, I spend my time in writing, skiing,
    painting too.
There's always just too much to do, and yet there's always
    something new.

I'm filled with love and thankful too.
I'm lucky having friends like you!

Because of all these disturbing feelings, I looked forward to
spending Christmas with the Walkers. Christmas Eve turned
out to be more dramatic than expected. We took Lou II and

Pill Pot out for a ride to see Christmas lights, so a neighbor would play Santa Claus by slipping in to put a match to a well-laid fire, showing that Santa had been there. We drove around for half an hour admiring colored lights and *farolitos* lining adobe fences and parapets, then headed home.

As we came down the driveway off Camino Santander, expecting to see bright-colored tree lights through the huge house window, all we could see was a faint glow of color through a deep gray smoke. Alarmed, Louie parked the car and ran into the house to find he'd forgotten to open the damper in the fireplace flue!

With doors open to air out smoke, we sat in coats, thankful there had been no serious damage. As we began opening gifts, Louie and Nicki eagerly awaited Lou II's excitement in opening a package containing a present they'd gone all-out to buy—tiny skis, bindings, and poles. Despite Santa's chimney episode, it was a Christmas to remember.

That summer, after my vague feelings about the necessity for a new direction in my life, major changes did occur in a serendipitous way. I unexpectedly joined the Unitarian Fellowship and met Tim Sanders, with whom I spent much of that summer. My friend and skiing partner Paul had had a skiing accident the previous winter, and had a cast on his leg. When Paul was grounded, he had introduced me to John Hernandez, who took over as my skiing companion. John's wife Frances sometimes came along and read in the ski lodge; but most of the time we went alone. Neither of us were great skiers; and I can still see John coming down the slopes with a wide grin on his face, an embroidered gray serape flying out behind him in the wind.

Late the last Saturday of the season as we were driving down the mountain on the way home John said, "Vi, Francie and I are going to a Unitarian Sunday service in Las Vegas tomorrow. Would you like to go along?"

I had always been interested in religion but had given up my childhood Lutheranism and not yet found a replacement. So I said to John, "Yes, I'd like to go," and he answered, "OK, I'll have Tim pick you up at 8:30." The next morning when I opened the door to Tim's knock, there stood a man about my height with red wavy hair and a shiny right-out-of-the-shower face. On the way back from Las Vegas, John and Francie invited us to stay for dinner at their home on the Las Vegas Highway outside of Santa Fe. But Tim had tickets for a foreign movie series, which didn't allow time for dinner, and he wanted me to come with him.

From then on, Tim and I attended Sunday services at the Unitarian Fellowship in Santa Fe, which he had joined when he came to Santa Fe from Texas. I saw a lot of him that summer. At first, I turned out to be a good listener as Tim seemed to need someone to hear his personal problems—the breakup of a marriage which had produced a son, together with his radical left-wing political beliefs. After Sunday services we often had dinner at John and Francie's sprawling adobe, where civil engineer John proudly showed us his design for special home water conservation—a system that allowed their bathwater to drain outside in the surrounding piñons.

The next year the Hernandezes introduced me to the world of Georgia O'Keeffe. They had bought an old ranch house near Abiquiu, New Mexico, close to Ghost Ranch, where I spent the weekend with them as they were renovating. On the way home to Santa Fe, we stopped at Georgia O'Keeffe's home. I remembered that Paul and Rebecca Strand had brought O'Keeffe to the early group Mabel Dodge Luhan had attracted to Taos. I liked the thought that I might meet O'Keeffe with my friends; but we did not find her at home that day when we drove down the winding road from Abiquiu.

John and Francie showed me the buildings behind a long wall that had belonged to an old Catholic mission which looked down from the crest of a mesa. O'Keeffe's house was on a flat stretch of red desert spotted with cactus, prickly pear, and sagebrush. On one side of the house was a canyon with a small circular cliff face about a hundred feet high with a chimney-shaped cliff at one end—all amidst colorful ancient rocks. O'Keeffe's beautiful plantings of flowers around the house reminded me of her flower paintings.

When I discovered O'Keeffe was a fellow Midwesterner, her pioneering qualities made me want to know more about her. I learned she had been born on a farm near Sun Prairie, Wisconsin, in 1887, where she lived until she was fifteen. Her artistic interests began there in Wisconsin before her family moved to Virginia.

It's a fascinating story of how her eastern school friend Anita Pollitzer brought her to the attention of New York's Alfred Stieglitz, who idolized and later married her. But it was while teaching in western Texas that Georgia found a place where she felt really at home and where she belonged. So when the Strands brought her to Mabel Dodge Luhan's group in Taos the summer of 1929, O'Keeffe was so enthralled with the land that after Stieglitz's death she decided to live in New Mexico and made it the most important part of the rest of her life.

To some people, O'Keeffe was aloof and austere, reflected in the isolation of her home, selectivity in friendships, and in her tall ramrod posture with her thin body dressed in black and white and anchored to the floor by flat shoes. By contrast, Mabel Dodge Luhan's lifestyle was colorful, sophisticated, and socially-oriented. Nevertheless, O'Keeffe found a good friend in Mabel's quiet nature-oriented Indian husband Tony, with whom she went on lengthy painting trips.

O'Keeffe's art always came from within, expressing our timeless struggles, polarities, and interrelations with nature. Some of this is expressed in her colorful flower portraits; and she also used such icons as stones and animal bones to express her powerful feelings about life.

In early years, O'Keeffe's abstract expressionism, combining European modernism and American energy, was criticized by those who did not wish to see women in the field. However,

George Goodrich, director emeritus of the Whitney Museum of American Art in New York, in sponsoring her exhibition at the Whitney in 1970, said that O'Keeffe had been a pioneer in art early in the game. Having grown up in Minnesota next to Wisconsin where O'Keeffe was born, I could always relate to her roots and her pioneering spirit, as well as to her fascination with northern New Mexico. Her special artistic expression conveyed that love of New Mexico to people around the world in a way that words could never do.

One of her paintings of northern New Mexico was recently selected to hang in the White House. Since her death in 1985, her house at Abiquiu has become a shrine for tourists and celebrities from around the world, as will the new Georgia O'Keeffe Museum, opened in 1997 in Santa Fe.

During this time my friendship with Tim began to deepen. I was always proud to be seen with Tim. Neat and pressed, in his ten-gallon Stetson and his western boots, he was ever ready for a TV commercial. He worked for a loan company in Santa Fe, where many Pueblo Indians had loans; and consequently he became good friends with some younger Indians, constantly urging them to keep up on their payments so as to avoid penalties and higher interest. Through Tim I learned more about Pueblo Indian culture, which profoundly interested him.

An Eric Hoffer True Believer, Tim tended to suppress parts of himself he did not like with campaigns for the underdog. The plight of the American Indian fascinated him; and he spent hours at the library reading whatever he could find about their history, to expand on what he had learned from knowing them personally.

I discovered that Tewa Indians lived in a world with many spirits. Throughout the year their complex calendar was based on positions of the sun and moon as days grew longer or shorter. According to their creation myth, they lived in a land between four sacred mountains of the Rio Grande Valley—one for each cardinal direction—with Sandia Crest in the south, the

Jemez Chicoma Peak in the west, Truchas Peak of the Sangre de Cristos in the east, and Canjilon Peak in the north. Each was associated with a color, an animal, a god, and a sacred lake.

I was fascinated by the fact that their concept of sexuality spoke to us in a simple, meaningful, mature manner. In their natural world, the male sun rose from the female earth and crossed the sky to the west to meet Mother Earth again at sunset. For this the Tewas offered thanks. Throughout the year, as days grew longer or shorter, the Tewas performed various dances near their ceremonial kivas to keep opposing spirits in balance—Mother Earth and Father Sun, the heat and rain for growing things in summer, the supply of wildlife in winter to feed their people during the year. At appropriate set times, they would move to the beat of drums as they performed such ceremonials as the Turtle Dance, the Buffalo Dance, the Eagle Dance, the Rainbow Dance, and the Corn Dance.

The plaza of each pueblo was the center of their ancient religion. There the *sipapu,* or spirit hole, was the place where the four sacred mountains came together. It led down to another universe—the world below, where the Cloud People, or Kachinas, lived and welcomed the souls of the dead. But Tim always emphasized that, according to his readings, even though the Tewas live in a world of spirits, they are not passive pawns of the gods, but rather a thankful working part of that spirit world, responsible for preserving its balance and control.

Because of Tim's deep friendships with some of his young Indian clients, who must have sensed his respect for Pueblo Indian traditions, he was invited by one of them from Santa Clara Pueblo to join in a ceremonial dance. Because I knew what a great honor this was (I had heard of only one other non-Indian having been given such an invitation), I did not point out how I felt—that in accepting, he was undermining the very traditions he was so strongly championing.

Although I would have loved to have learned what happened in the kiva, I knew that had to be secret. Tim did say later that he sensed resentment of his presence by some of the elders in the kiva as they painted up and went through their secret ceremonies. I could surely understand this; for I think I'd have been on their side.

I promised Tim I'd be at Santa Clara Pueblo to take pictures of the dancing. It was a cloudy cold spring day with patches of snow on the ground as I joined many other tourists to watch. After the secret kiva ceremony, the dancers came out naked, except for loincloths, with much of their body painted gray, white, and black with a bit of red. As they danced in a long row, a couple in front of me, looking at the Indians one by one down the line, did a big double-take as they came to the red-headed man at least half a head shorter than the others. I always wondered what they said later. It was a time to remember for both Tim and I, but it had an unfortunate ending for him. Although he was a bodybuilder who regularly worked out with weights, because of the weather and exposure Tim ended up in bed with pneumonia.

Tim often talked of his Uncle Bill from Texas, who had been one of the original cowboys with the famed Matador Ranch. That summer, during one such conversation, we realized that stories like Uncle Bill's should be written down and published. So Tim invited his uncle to Santa Fe to start writing his memoirs.

When Uncle Bill arrived, he was a man of slight build with a wry smile, and so soft spoken one had to listen carefully as he told his tales. Teasing me, Tim once said, "See Vi, not all Texans are loud!" Uncle Bill could go back to early days at the Matador Ranch, relating tales of cattle runs from Texas to Montana which took months, sometimes running into winter weather when cattle froze to death on the trail. He told how the ownership of the Matador Ranch changed and an American finally had to get money from a financier in Scotland, who purchased the 840,000 acres. According to Uncle Bill, it was the cowboys themselves who founded the town of Matador. To legally qualify, a town had to have twenty business establishments, so the cowboys set up some, including a grocery store with some cans on a shelf, a dry goods store with a few bolts of material on a counter, and a hardware store with fence posts and other useful items—actually creating the town with its famous post office.

I still treasure a weekend the three of us spent on a camping trip along a stream in Santa Barbara Canyon. In the evening I had a tiff with Tim, who had taken off to his sleeping bag. After that I sat at the fire with Uncle Bill, watching the sparks rise up between the slender spires of the tallest aspen trees I can remember. Although I knew nothing about his kind of ranch life, and no doubt did ask silly questions, he responded with tales I felt honored to hear. As time passed, his voice got softer and softer. I had to edge closer and closer till we were nearly head to head. Some weeks later Uncle Bill sent a handwritten letter from the famous town he'd help found:

Matador, Texas, August 19, 1957

Dear Vi,

It has been real hot here since I came back until day before yesterday when a light norther blew in.

It's hard work for anyone who hasn't used their ninth grade education for fifty years or more, but my plans for the book would be to make a paper back one and price them at about one cent a page. I think they would sell good in these small towns, and in the larger places also. If this printing machine Timothy mentioned operates OK and doesn't cost too much we might make the books ourselves and not be obligated to any publishing co.

Best wishes and thanks for the photo. W.W.

I was pleased that Tim had made my summer more interesting by introducing me to Uncle Bill. He seemed then, and even more today, a wonderful example of the simple people from yesteryear.

True Believer Tim often spoke of becoming a lawyer, so he

could take on cases of the disadvantaged. Although he did have an undergraduate degree, law school would require at least three more years and expenditures for a library. What is more, he would have to make a name for himself before he could afford to work for people who couldn't pay legal fees. I kept pointing this out to him; and when I learned that many Unitarian churches were oriented toward socially conscious action, I suggested that he should think of becoming a Unitarian minister. Then, after three years of graduate school, he could begin the kind of work he wanted to do.

Tim didn't think much of my idea until he was transferred to the Albuquerque office of his firm, and found that Dr. Smith, the Unitarian minister there, was involved in both the American Civil Liberties Union and the NAACP. This involvement made the idea of the ministry most attractive; and eventually Tim applied to Harvard Divinity School in Boston and to Starr King School for the Ministry in Berkeley.

Tim was fascinated when he heard that the Berkeley school was named after Thomas Starr King, the Unitarian minister in San Francisco who was credited with saving California for the Union during the Civil War. Along with Father Serra, who founded all the Catholic missions along the West Coast, Thomas Starr King was one of the Californians chosen for the Hall of Fame in our Washington, D.C., capital, back when states could pick their two leading citizens.

During this time, Tim came up to Santa Fe most weekends to continue our affair. But for me the experience was ever marred by Tim's True Believer traits, which were so well described in Howard Fast's novel *The UnAmericans*. It was set in Los Alamos, with the heroine admonishing her boyfriend that he was so in love with his cause that he had no love left for anyone.

That fall Tim was admitted to Starr King School for the Ministry, and I drove to Berkeley with him. We spent the first night out in Las Vegas, where thanks to Tim's insistence, we saw the unique entertainer Jimmy Durante at the Painted

Desert Room—at that time "America's smartest supper club."

Before flying back to work in Santa Fe, I spent a day with my Red Cross friend in Berkeley. During the flight home, I reflected on my relationship with Tim, realizing that he still had not come to terms with a Texas divorce involving his son, and that he had suppressed this lack of resolution in Santa Fe by promoting causes for the Tewa Indians. Then he had joined the Unitarian Church in Albuquerque, where Dr. Smith had offered new outlets for his crusading. But still, despite his shortcomings, and because I had been more than intellectually involved with Tim, I missed him more than I thought I would. And his departure seemed to foreshadow my own impending lifestyle change suggested in my Christmas card that year to friends:

> And as for me, I go along,
> in pleasant ruts I've been too long,
> just waiting for some motivation
> to change the place or occupation.

CHAPTER 10

Leaving Santa Fe: From the Land of Enchantment to Unitarianism

With Tim in Berkeley, I had more time to participate in activities with old friends, such as going on a long weekend camping trip to the rim of the Grand Canyon with rockhound friend Pat Insley. We went to see Winnie Foster, the widow of a dentist who had worked for the Indian Service. Winnie had gone to the bottom of the canyon with her husband when he worked on the teeth of Indians there. She was known and loved by all the Indians of that area.

We set up camp on the edge of the canyon. After eating, we went up to the gift shop in a nearby park building. It had a balcony overlooking a breathtaking view of the canyon at sunset. Later, while looking for possible gifts to take back, Winnie exclaimed, "Oh! that's George!" pointing to a large glossy portrait of a handsome Indian on a bulletin board. "It surely is," said the clerk. "Where's George now?" Winnie asked. "Oh, he's shoeshine boy over at El Tovar," the clerk replied.

We immediately went on to El Tovar, the big lodge where we found George with a bright orange band around his head, accenting a big black eye. Winnie ran up and said, "George, what happened to you?" He grinned. "Oh, Mrs. Foster, I was out at the pueblo for the Shalako—that ceremony when we celebrate all the new houses that have been built and they have pole climbing and throw food and gifts from the top of the pole. That night I got hit with a can of peaches!"

On that canyon trip, I learned that Winnie was booked for a freighter trip around the world. I was fascinated and sent for all the information to join her, with the thought that it would be a good way to make the break from my beloved Santa Fe I kept talking about but never could quite act on. However, when I learned the ship had a berth only as far as Hong Kong, I pictured myself there on the beach, thumbing my way home, and gave up on the idea. Still, thinking of Indians and Tim's departure kept reminding me of my own restlessness and need for a change.

With weekends free, at this time my friend Paul came back into my life. Once my skiing companion, he now joined me for weekly trips to the Ski Basin. The first time we had along the teenage son of friends; and on the way back, as Paul dropped me at my apartment and I asked him in for a drink to thank him for the trip, he said, "No thanks, Vi, I'd better get Jack home." I somehow knew, however, that the next time Jack would not be along and Paul would accept my invitation.

Paul and I had wonderful times at the mountain. He reminded me of a boyfriend, Andy, I had known during World War II. Andy and I had met on my leave to the Riviera, and he later got transfers so he could come to Garmisch, where I had taught him to ski. But I had to end my relationship with Andy because of our age difference. My friendship with Paul was also problematic. Because he was married and I knew his wife, I had to close the door to any relationship, although we did spend hours talking in the car about deep aspects of love and life. Today, I still treasure the closeness we experienced as Paul once said, "Vi, you know more about me than any other human on this earth."

More and more the thoughts that I should leave my Santa Fe Shangri-la seemed to surface. There was ever the feeling that life was short and in a human lifetime one could only begin to tap its myriad possibilities. As a single person, it was only my decision, and I was getting increasingly restless. But then I would think of how much I loved the summers in my pink and blue country of rolling piñon-covered hills, with mountains rising on both sides of the Rio Grande Valley, winters of skiing on the mountain, and all my wonderful friends. Where could I find another a place that could match this?

Finally, in September 1958 I began to explore the possibility of going to Berkeley, and wrote my Red Cross friend who was an interior decorator there. She sent a card immediately, saying, "Delighted to hear from you. It's been a long time. And even happier to learn that I may see you soon. Of course you can stay with me as long as you can or want to!"

I also wrote Easton Rothwell, my mentor from college days at Reed College in Portland, Oregon, who was then director of the Hoover Institution on War, Revolution, and Peace at Stanford University: "Even though years go by and you hear nothing from me but a Merry Christmas, both you and Virginia have been touchstones for me all these years. How often I've thought of my Washington visit when you were at the State Department, and tried to get me to work there. I was so upset with what you told me, I said, Easton, don't you want to tell them to take their job! You said to me over a glass of rye in your Arlington apartment, 'You're a smart girl, Vi, but there's one thing that one day you'll have to learn—and that's that we do not make the world over, over night!'"

I then went on to share my feelings about leaving Santa Fe to come to Berkeley. I remarked:

> I've dug myself another wonderfully comfortable rut, but feel that after almost ten years in Santa Fe, it's time to move on. I love this place and the country around here and all my friends; but though the art colony atmosphere is stimulating in myriad ways, it's almost like being on a continual vacation.
>
> Though I haven't given up the hope that I'll not always have to support myself, I do feel in the meantime I might find someone or something that could tax my abilities and ingenuity a bit more. In my present spot I'm spoiled, as the single gal in the office and among my married friends, and I'm afraid I've become very selfish.
>
> I have a yearning to do more than I'm doing—something that will be of some significance on my record one day—not for glory, but because I know I have much

God-given potential I've not even tapped. So just to get myself started in that direction, I've thought of you, to see whether by any chance you know of some interesting person or cause I might tie in with in your part of the country.

In a long letter he typed at home, Easton counseled me to give serious thought to my relationship with Tim, which I had mentioned, and suggested that I take a leave of absence and come to Berkeley, offering to introduce me to people who could be of help. He continued, "As you know, Vi, the big city is far different from your beloved Santa Fe; but I can set up appointments with people who would appreciate the wonderful help you could be for them. And for you I feel it shouldn't be back into some university position." He was sure I would find congenial friends and said he shared my admiration of the Unitarians and American Friends programs—that indeed just after he had finished his undergraduate work at Reed he had spent a year as assistant to Dr. Eliot, Minister of the Portland Unitarian Church, whom he admired.

After some weeks of pondering, I wrote Easton, thanking him for his invitation and advice but telling him I had decided against a leave of absence, feeling that if I were going to make a break, it should be clean—so that I couldn't go back. Although I'd always treasure my ten years in Santa Fe, they had been almost too comfortable. I wished to find a whole new world, though I was not sure how or where. I looked forward to seeing Tim, with whom I'd kept in touch, but also to making new friends. And with my years of experience as a secretary and then office manager at the Santa Fe Chamber of Commerce, I did not need to worry about finding work. I kept wondering more about the possible new friends—both male and female—and what future such a change would bring.

Ultimately I did tell Kenneth Clark of my wish to leave, promising to stay on through February to handle the examinations by the Board of Examiners for Architects of New

Mexico, of which he was head, but for which I did most of the work. Then even though I'd made the decision to leave, I kept telling friends who asked that I was still waiting for letters from my Berkeley friends.

Even though I had told Kenneth Clark I was leaving, he did nothing about finding a replacement so I finally called an employment agency, which sent two applicants. The first was a plump woman with severely marcelled dark brown hair, dressed in a navy blue suit—the epitome of efficiency. Later that afternoon, the second applicant arrived—a tall, slender woman in a tight black skirt and white blouse, her glossy black hair drawn back in a low chignon. As she walked by the archway to the drafting room, I heard low whistles from the men.

Later, when Kenneth called me in. I was aware of an uncharacteristic grin on his face as he said, "Vi, Miss A surely looked capable; but I think perhaps we should hire her to do the work, and Miss B for the front office." I also grinned as I retorted, "Kenneth Clark, I've done it all for you for how many years, and you know I'm no glamour puss!" He just kept smiling.

One evening I was working at the office when Paul trailed me there about nine. After talking for nearly an hour, we went to my apartment for a drink. Paul did not want me to move to Berkeley, and felt I should take a leave of absence before making such a decision. I explained my feelings, saying, "But, Paul, I truly believe that when I make a break that should be it, so I can't come back." Finally, he agreed, and our conversation turned to the new Vi, how I should adapt to the big city, and what my future would be like. It was a night I shall always remember.

My friend Ethel had a farewell party for me at her home a few miles out of Santa Fe near Tesuque. It was just a day before I was to leave; and it had snowed that night. As friends were leaving, Paul said, "Vi, you can't go tomorrow. There's new powder up at the Ski Basin. We've just got to have one more time up there together." I was all packed, had left my apartment, and had one more day with Ethel. Paul picked me up there the next day, and after our last nostalgic time on the mountain, we returned late afternoon, knowing that Ethel would be away at work.

Although I was excited with the prospects of new adventure in Berkeley, my decision to leave Santa Fe was closing the book on ten years of an extraordinary living experience. I thought of the colorful early history of that tiny part of our world I had not even been told about at school. I recalled the many times I had walked the sunny streets of Santa Fe under azure skies and joyously reminded myself "This is my home!" And I remembered the evenings I would cross the bridge onto Canyon Road, turning left into the drive and down to the car-port along the Santa Fe River then looking up at the touchable stars to say to my still unbelieving self, "I live here!"

While living in Santa Fe during the 1950s, I felt I had truly experienced why it was known as the City Different. And although I deplore the changes brought about by questionable growth, who am I to question the feelings that still draws others to the Land of Enchantment. As we frantically rush to the world of the Internet, with ecological concerns, battles of political power, and distributions of wealth around our world, I can only hope that the thousands of people now flocking to Santa Fe each year might be touched with the magic found there many years ago by individuals such as Mabel Dodge Luhan and D. H. Lawrence.

After testing the boundaries of human relationships and values of their time as wealthy intellectuals, they found in northern New Mexico the profound yet simple life meanings they had sought earlier around the world. They found it in Tony Luhan's world of the Tewa Indians at Taos Pueblo—with their respect for the lessons of our natural world, in which there is no race for money, fame, and power. And even though Mabel Dodge Luhan's big house in Taos is now an expensive B & B and tourist attraction, she remains for me a pioneering spirit who fearlessly lived her dreams.

Lately, I have become hopeful about the future while reading George Johnson's 1995 *Fire in the Mind: Science, Faith,
and the Search for Order.*[*] This science editor for the *New
York Times* came from the big city to visit his home region of
northern New Mexico. In driving the back road from Santa
Fe to Taos—past pueblos with kivas, the Lourdes of America
at Chimayo, Penitentes' *moradas* in Spanish villages—these
centers of ancient religions spoke to him in a new way. He
thought of the secret religious ceremonies of the Indians
and Spanish which had given meaning to their worlds and lives
for centuries.

His mind then wandered to events he recalled occurring
across the Rio Grande Valley. He thought of blue and white
plastic signs he had seen cautioning DANGER/EXPLO-
SIVES/KEEP OUT in canyons and on mesa tops around Los
Alamos, remembering how what had happened there had
changed our world forever in ways we still don't fully comprehend.

Then, on the way home in the foothills just north of the city
he passed an outgrowth of Los Alamos—the Institute of Santa
Fe. There a walled home shelters New Age scientists seeking
laws of ever-more complexity to explain how our universe gives
rise to life, mind, and society of our world.

In entertaining these thoughts, Johnson wondered about
the polarities as well as future possibilities. A community that
had expressed itself in the arts and religions of Indian, Spanish,
and Anglo cultures over the centuries, had now also become a
city of science. In commenting on its portrayal of northern
New Mexico, Paul Davies views Johnson's book as "A must for
all those seriously interested in the key ideas at the frontier of
scientific discourse." On the dust jacket he says:

---

[*] George Johnson, *Fire in the Mind: Science, Faith, and the Search for
Order* (New York: Alfred Knopf, 1984).

Northern New Mexico is home both to the most provocative new enterprises in quantum physics, information science, and the evolution of complexity and to the cosmologies of the Tewa Indians and the Catholic Penitentes. As it draws the reader into this landscape, juxtaposing the systems of belief that have taken root there, *Fire in the Mind* develops into a gripping intellectual adventure story that compels us to ask where science ends and religion begins.

Johnson had the background and stature to express something I had long questioned and frequently discussed with male students at my theological school—our excessive rational, scientific approach to much of life and living. I had always felt that other peoples, like American Indians, centuries ago recognized another dimension in the intangible essence of human beings that cannot be measured in numbers. It was comforting to know that some individuals with a notable scientific background felt the same way.

Today, I often think back to my beloved Santa Fe of the 1950s but now with new questions and ideas to consider. I'll forever treasure my Santa Fe years and friends up and down the Rio Grande Valley between the Sangre de Cristos and the Jemez Mountains in the Land of Enchantment.

In the summer of 1959, I left Santa Fe in a loaded Studebaker Landcruiser with a ski carrier on top holding folding chairs in case I rented an unfurnished apartment in Berkeley. Had anyone said then that I was headed for the Unitarian ministry, I would have told them they were dreaming. At the time I didn't even know a woman could become a minister.

On the way to Berkeley, I stopped to see friends in Phoenix, Los Angeles, and Santa Barbara, and we'd sit up half the night talking about what I should do with the rest of my life. They came up with crazy ideas such as advising me to buy a red convertible and see the whole country; but they also cautioned me about moving to the big city after living in the Santa Fe I seemed to love so much.

When I arrived in Berkeley, I found that my Red Cross friend's interior decorating studio was only a block and a half from Starr King School for the Ministry, where Tim was a student. He took me to some parties at the school; and in meeting and talking with other students and faculty, I became fascinated with the curriculum—not at all what one would expect at a theological school. The catalog said:

> Course offerings give attention to emergent issues in ethics, social justice, gender studies, and theology. Starr King consistently includes courses in spirituality, world religions, Unitarian Universalist history, education, and practical arts of ministry.

As a result, through serendipitous events, I was admitted to this graduate school as a special student, since I had not completed my undergraduate degree. I feel sure the president never expected me to wish to graduate; but I didn't want to be a teacher or a nurse or even a secretary, and the prospect of becoming a minister was exciting. To help with expenses, I got a part-time job on the nearby University of California campus.

The men students at school were wonderfully supportive, and three years later I became the first woman graduate of Starr King School for the Ministry, receiving a certificate of completion since I'd been admitted without my undergraduate degree. After serving as minister for many years, when colleges started giving credit for experience, the faculty at Starr King School for the Ministry recommended to their Board of Trustees that I be granted a Master of Divinity degree retroactively to 1962. As a result, I received two diplomas with a letter explaining that the engraver of the first had not realized the gender of the recipient and had said, "completed *his* program," so he made a second. Now I tell friends I have two master's degrees, a "his" and a "hers."

As my friend Easton had suggested, I gave serious thought to breaking off my relationship with Tim. The first months of trying didn't work; but again through serendipity we were once again separated—this time for good. Tim became involved with a cause which changed his life—this time with a group of Trotskyites who were enamored with Trotsky's program of world revolution, which had resulted in Trotsky's expulsion from Russia by Stalin. Tim's new cause kept him from registering for the second semester at Starr King School for the Ministry, and he left Berkeley. I missed him but later realized how the relationship had not only been a learning experience for me but had brought me to Berkeley and the Unitarian ministry. I am constantly amazed at how seemingly insignificant decisions can change the direction of one's life.

During the fifteen years after graduation from Starr King School for the Ministry, I served as minister to four Unitarian churches: at Provincetown, Massachusetts, out on the tip of Cape Cod; at Calgary, Alberta, in the shadow of the Canadian Rockies (where I was the first woman Unitarian minister in Canada; at Tallahassee, Florida, in the Deep South; and at Kent, Ohio.

My ministries always attracted youth, two of whom have become proud protégés of mine in the ministry. In addition to my commitment to bringing the spiritual dimension to both women and men, I feel historically my ministries were startlingly prophetic by encompassing controversial social and political issues still with us today, including gay and lesbian rights, the Vietnam War, civil rights, reproductive rights, and the disintegration of the family.

Throughout my ministries I felt that I had much to give from my decade of living in the beautiful high country of Santa Fe, where I learned the early history of my country involving Spanish and Indian cultures, and had scientist friends at Los Alamos, the birthplace of our history-making atomic world. All these experiences took place in a unique natural setting that attracted independent, creative souls. I now like to think I was one of them—in sharing what I learned in Santa Fe with many people throughout the United States.

Since retirement, I have become known as a writer. The University Press of Kentucky published my *One Woman's World War II*, a story of my experiences directing military on-base service clubs in England under buzz bombs before D-Day. On the Continent, as senior club director for the 82nd Airborne, I was with this division as we liberated a concentration camp, and met and celebrated with the Russians after General Gavin accepted surrender of the 21st German Army. In Berlin, I was a dinner guest of General Eisenhower. It was felt my book was special because it was a woman's story of the war. In August 1996, Boston's Skinner House Books published *A Modern Pioneer: One Woman's Ministry*. On the dust jacket it said:

> The first woman to graduate from Starr King School for the Ministry, Violet Kochendoerfer looks back on her remarkable life and accomplishments. Her sermons, articles and correspondence become startlingly prophetic in historical perspective. Each of Kochendoerfer's ministries tackled controversial social and political issues that soon define a dynamic era in American history—gay and lesbian rights, the Vietnam War, civil rights, reproductive rights, and the disintegration of the family. Always on the cutting edge, Kochendoerfer's ministry helped liberal religion respond to the key events of her generation.

Santa Fe in the Fifties covers the ten years in between these two books, and I'm beginning a fourth—*Growing Up in Minnesota: Depression and All*. Often I have said that one lifetime is too brief to begin to experience the endless possibilities for self-expression and service to others. So, thinking about the past, I'm glad that I did leave my beloved Santa Fe to discover other experiences—first in the Unitarian ministry and then as an author. All of these recent activities were deeply influenced by my life in Santa Fe of the 1950s. And now, with ever new ideas and questions to consider in our new society, I'll forever treasure the unique wisdom of my Santa Fe experiences, and friends up and down the Rio Grande Valley between the Sangre de Cristos and the Jemez Mountains in the Land of Enchantment.